Glimpses of Germany

FROM BAVARIA TO BERLIN

A TRAVEL PHOTO ART BOOK

LAINE CUNNINGHAM

Glimpses of Germany
From Bavaria to Berlin
A Travel Photo Art Book

Published by Sun Dogs Creations
Changing the World One Book at a Time
Print ISBN: 9781946732828

Cover Design by Angel Leya

Copyright © 2018 Laine Cunningham

THE TRAVEL PHOTO ART SERIES

Bikes of Berlin

Necropolises of New Orleans I & II

Ruins of Rome I & II

Ancients of Assisi I & II

Panoramas of Portugal

Nuances of New York

Glimpses of Germany

Impressions of Italy

Utopia of the Unicorn

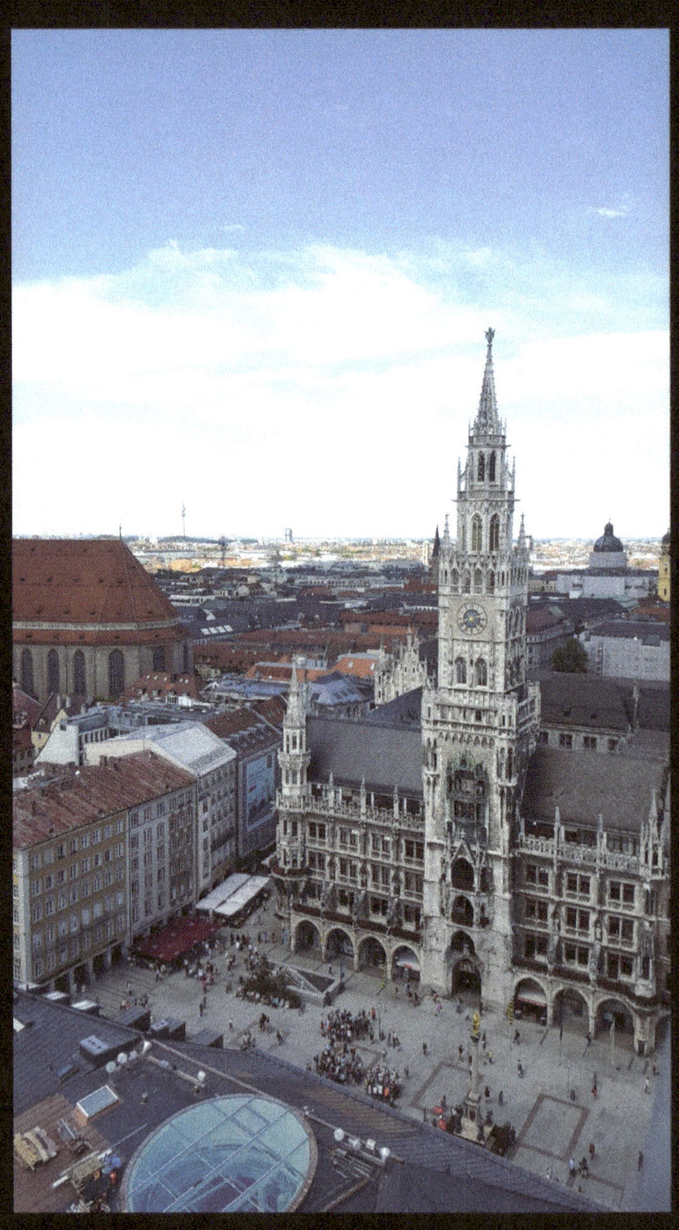

DONJON

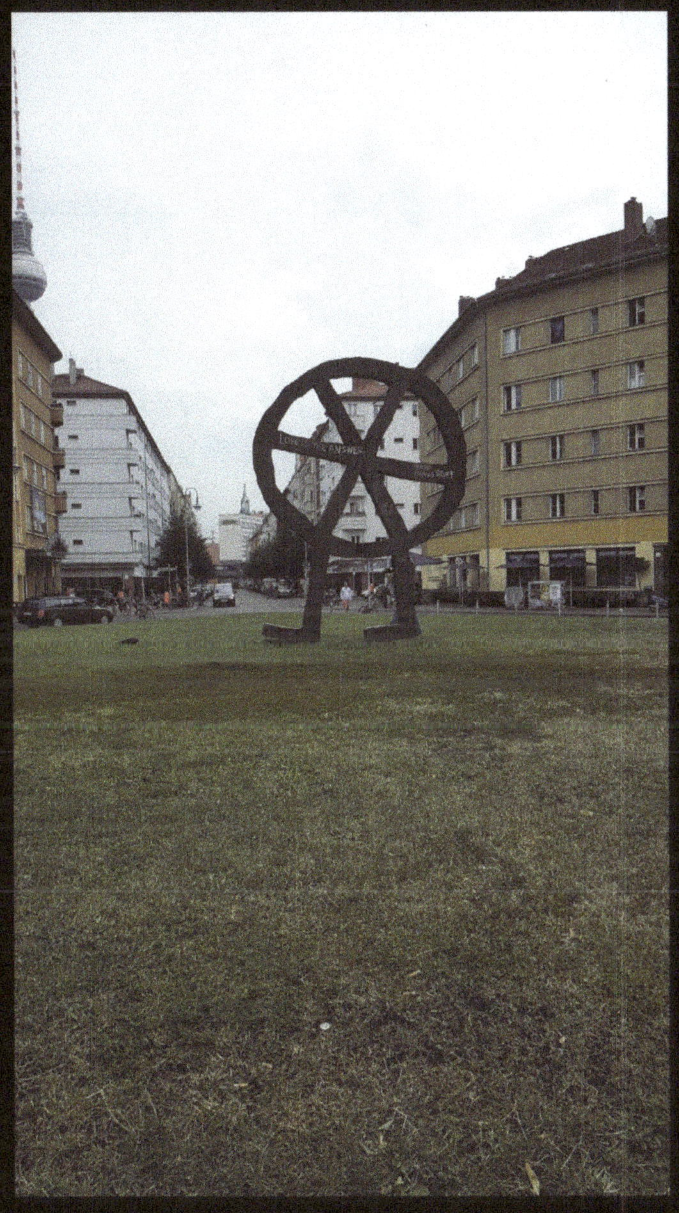

WALKING WHEEL

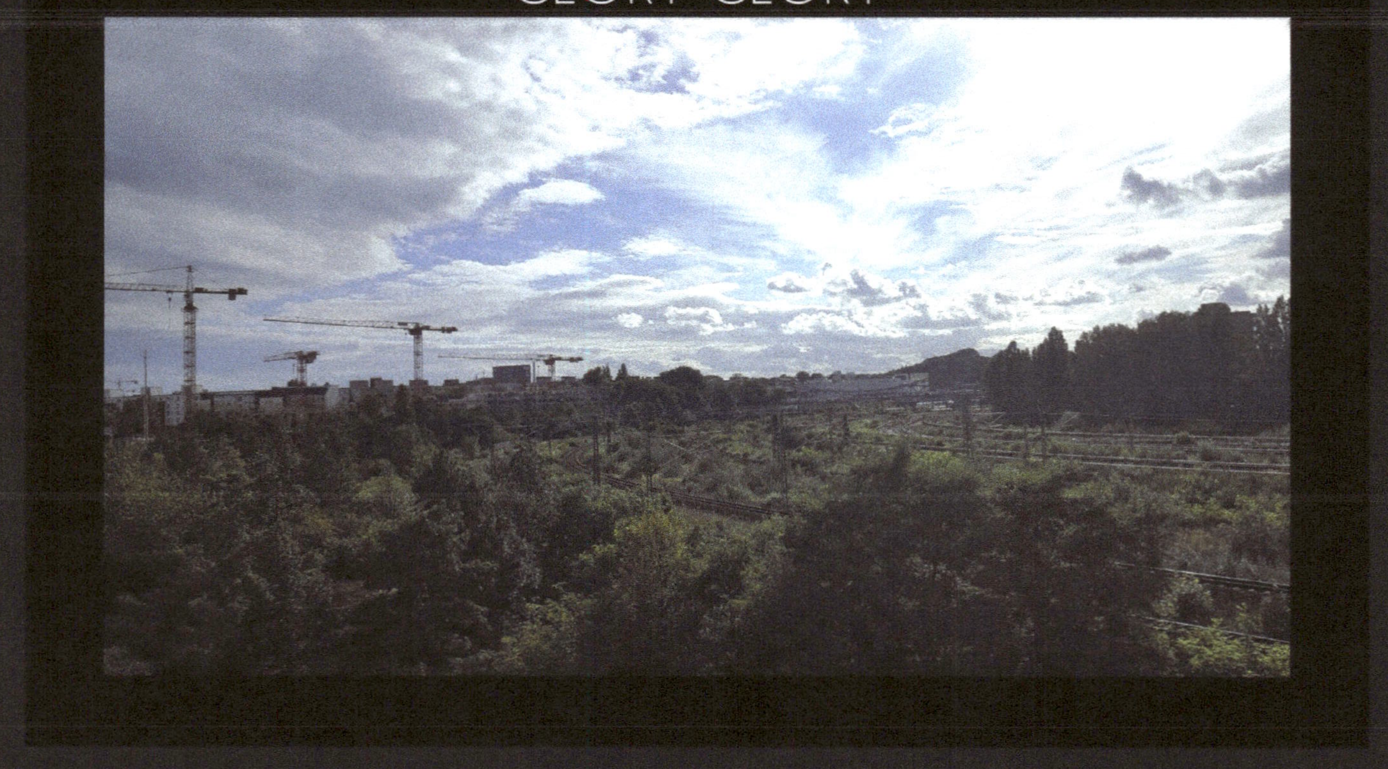
GLORY GLORY

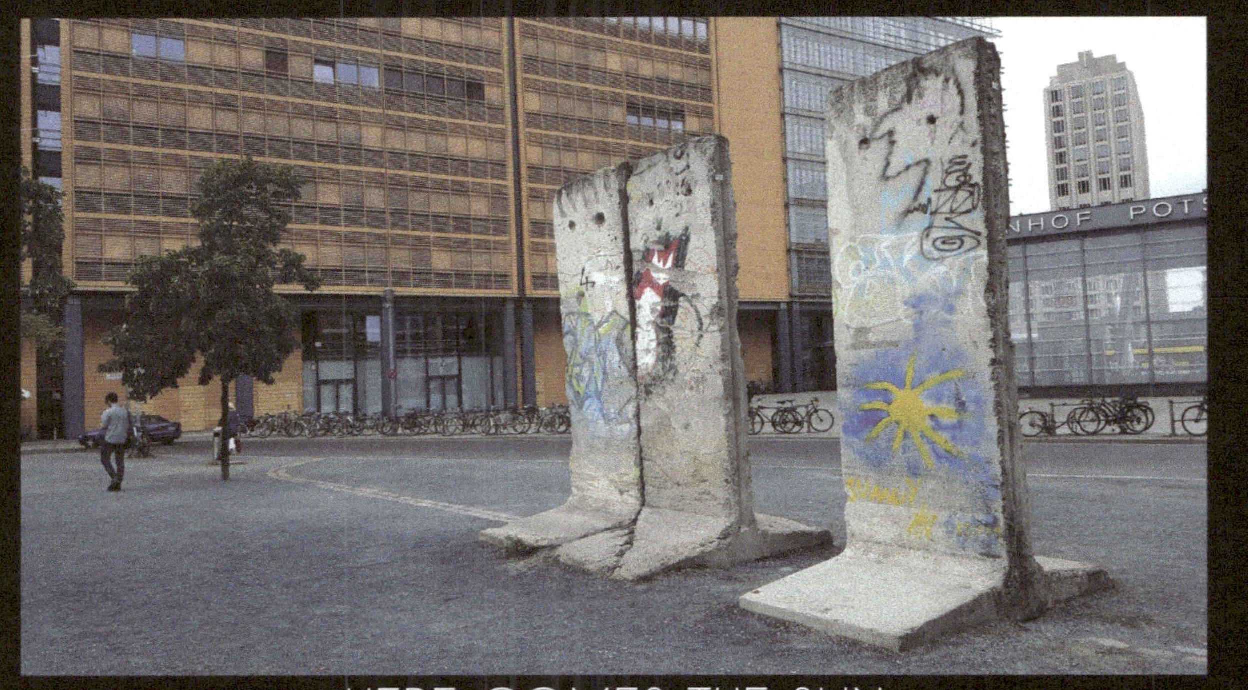

HERE COMES THE SUN

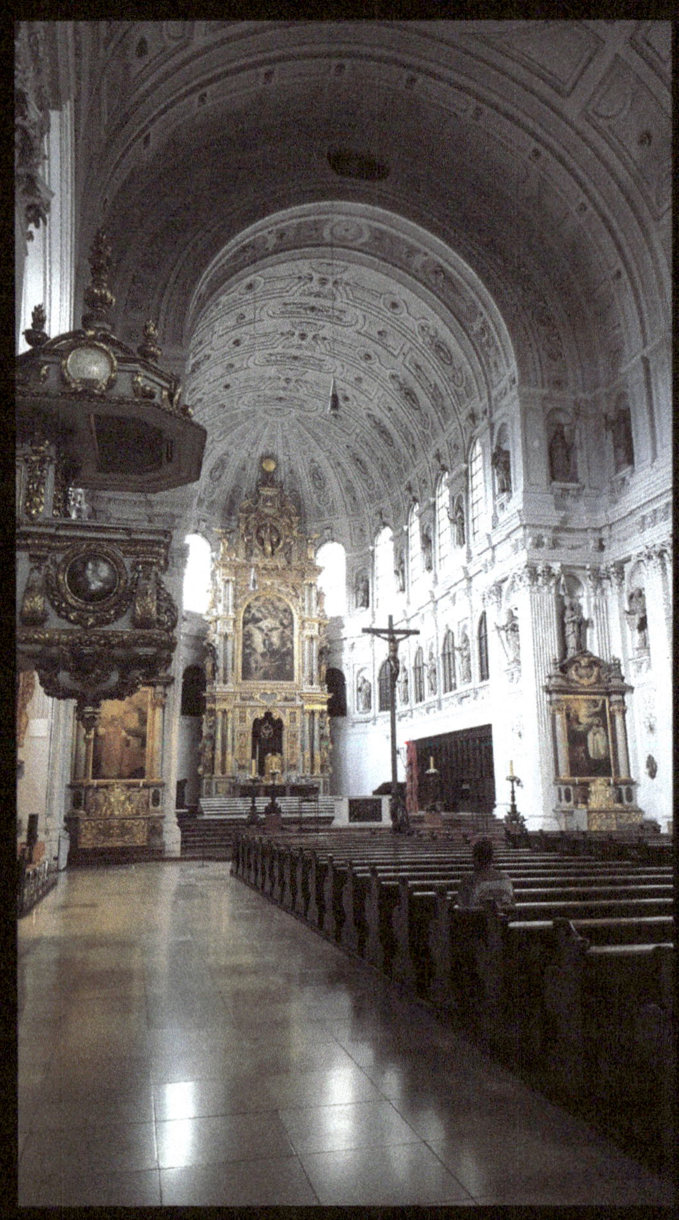

MEDITATION

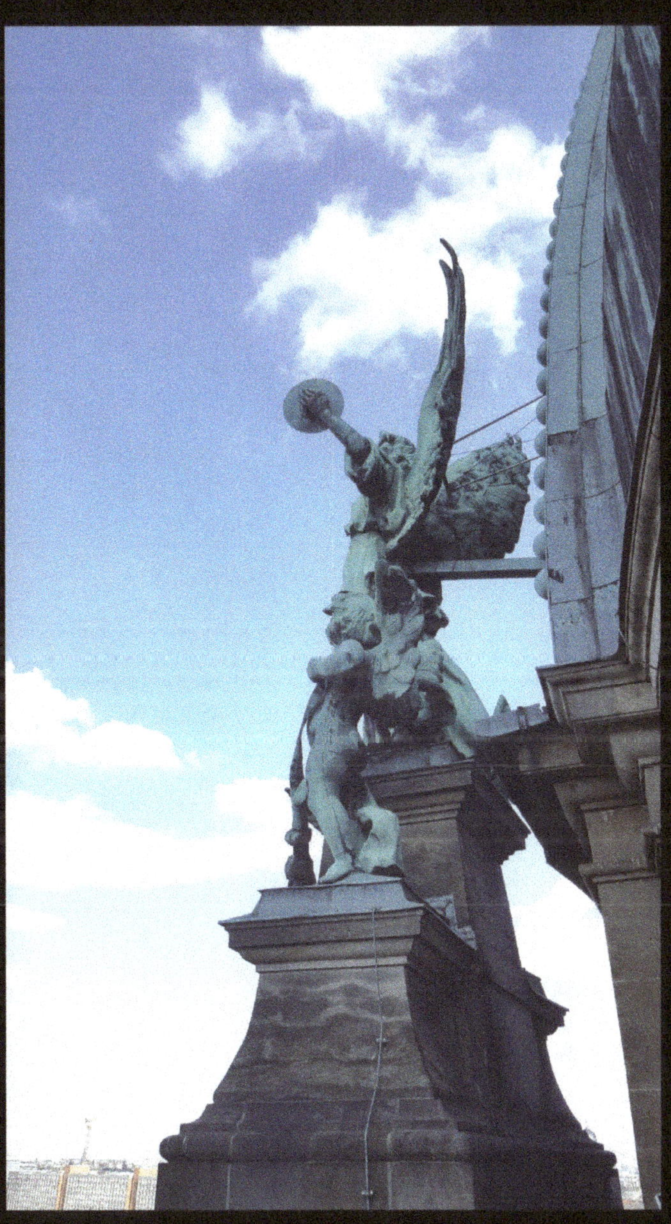

MAJESTIC

LOW BRIDGE

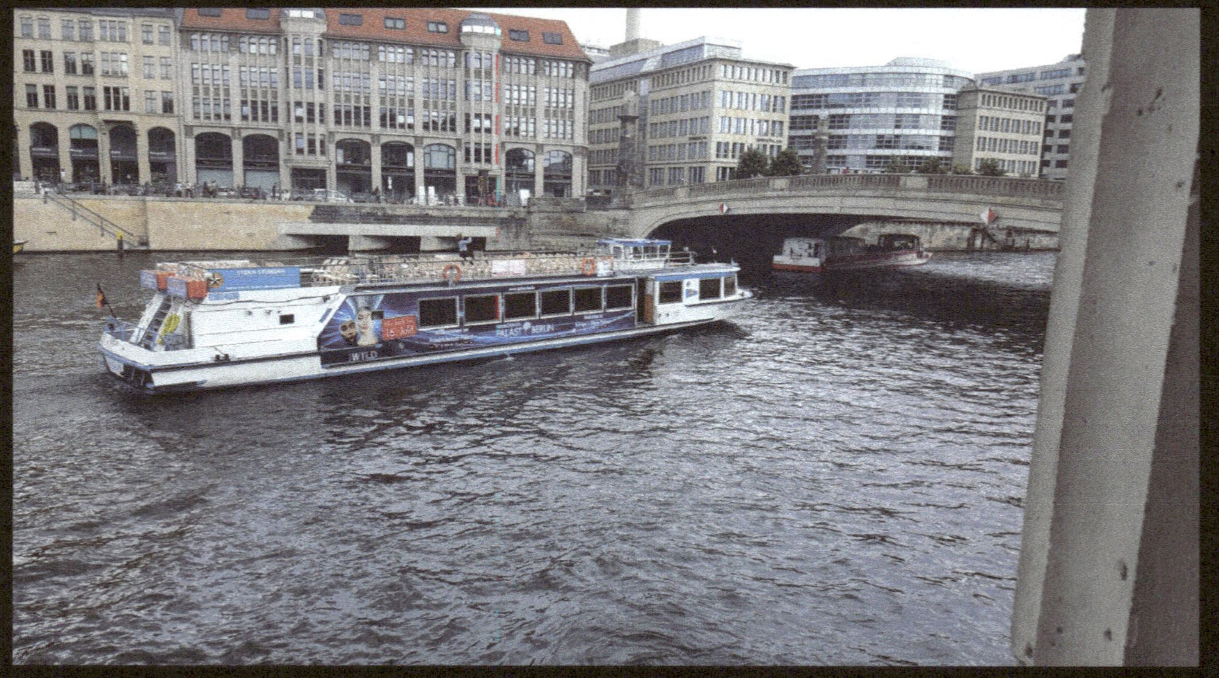

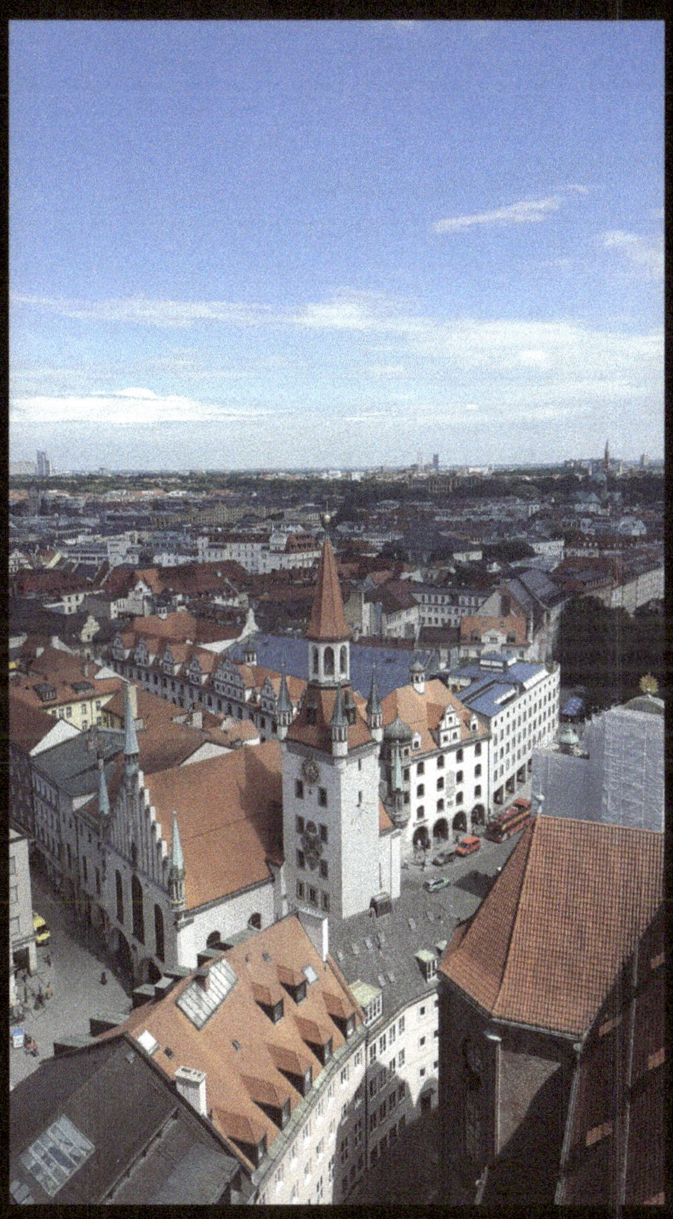

PICTURE POSTCARD

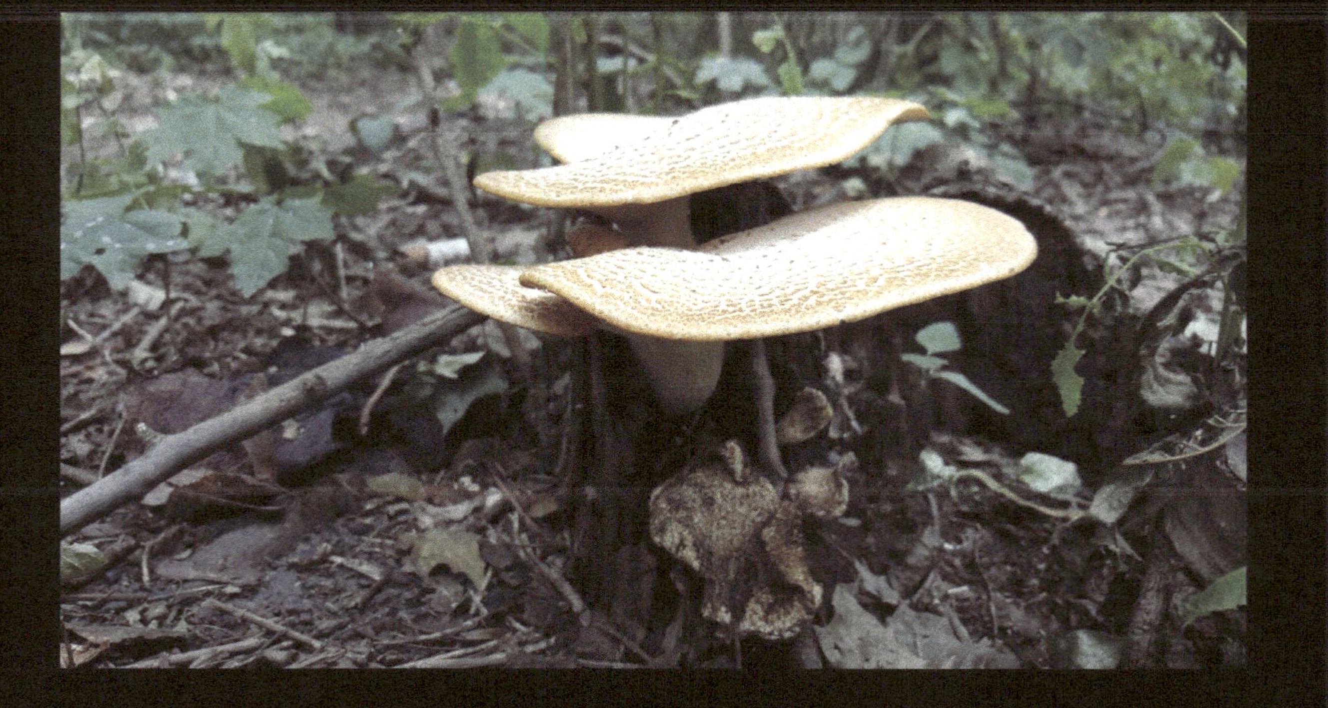

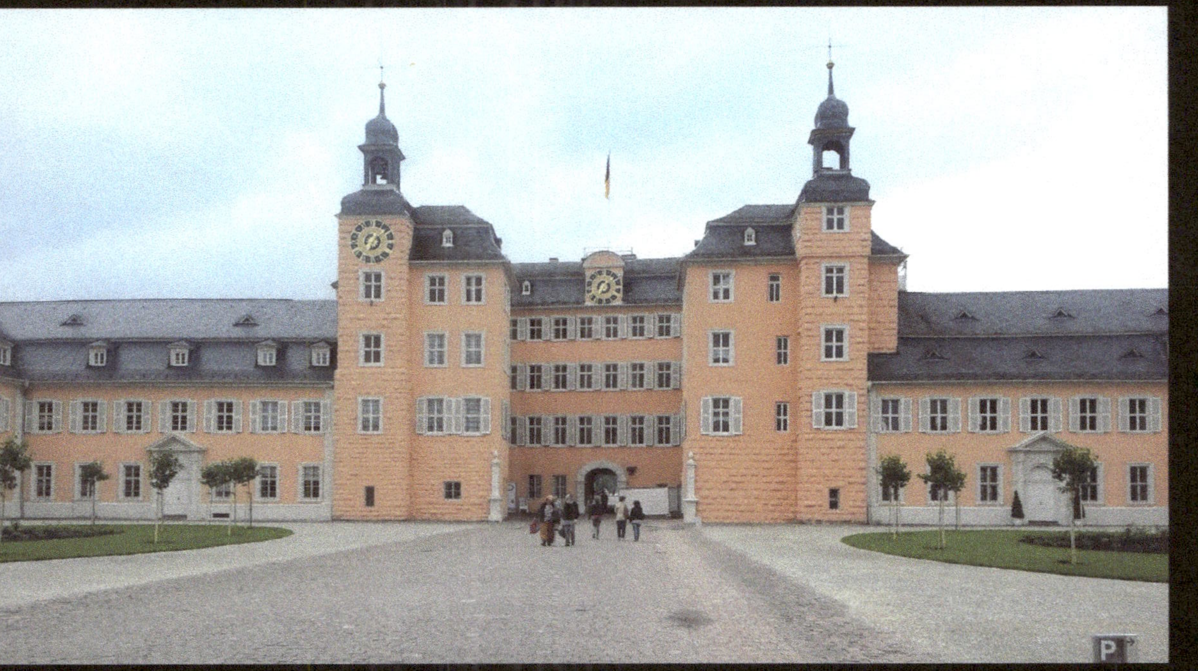
SHERBET

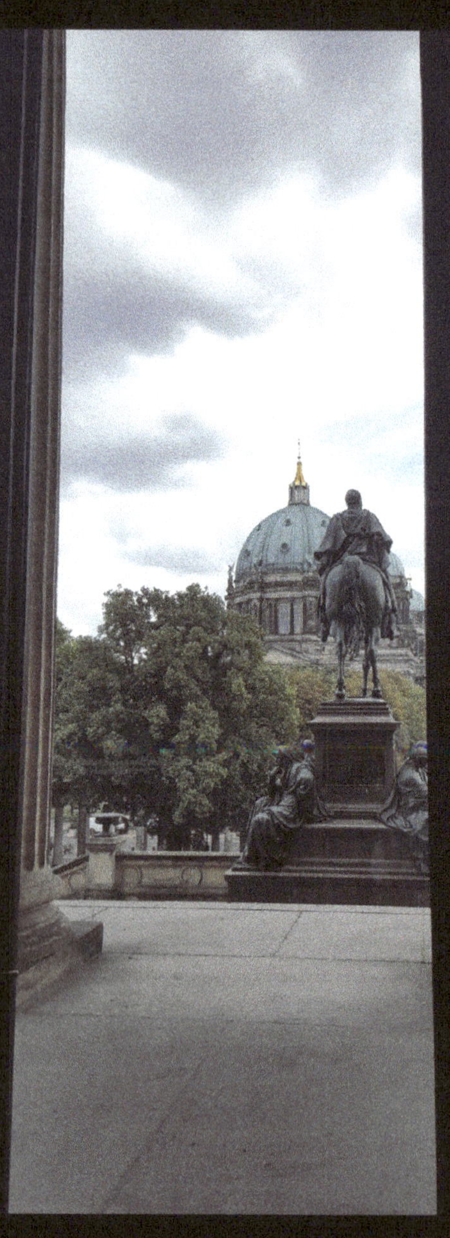

THROUGH THE LOOKING GLASS

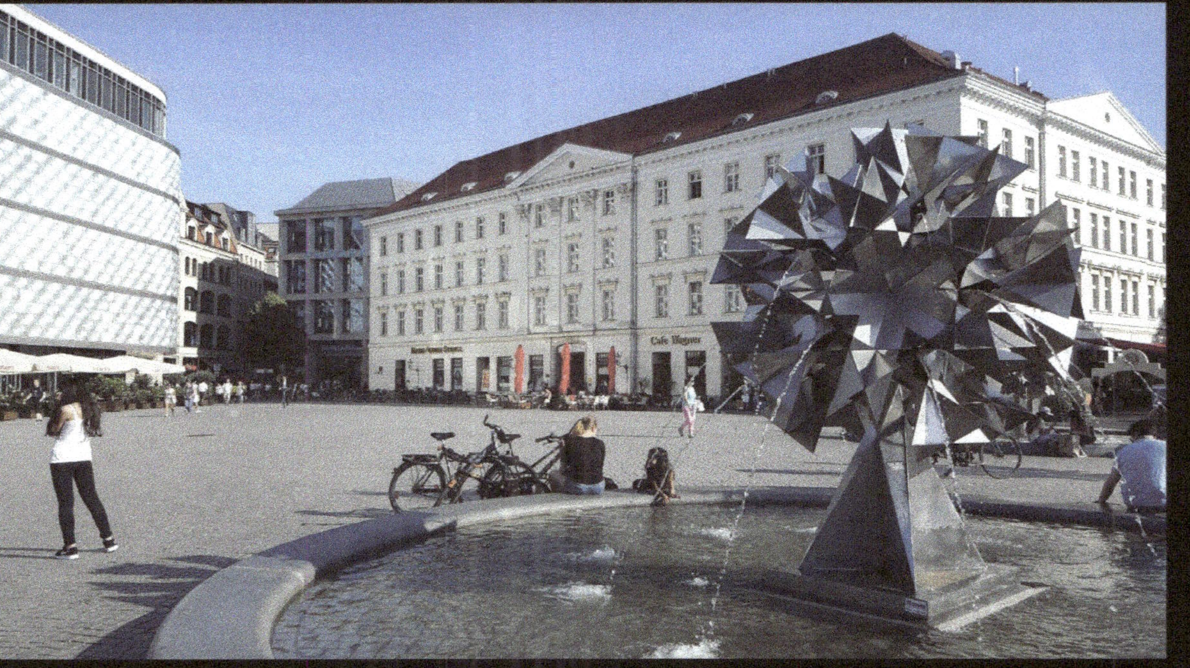

TUMBLEWEED

WONDERLAND

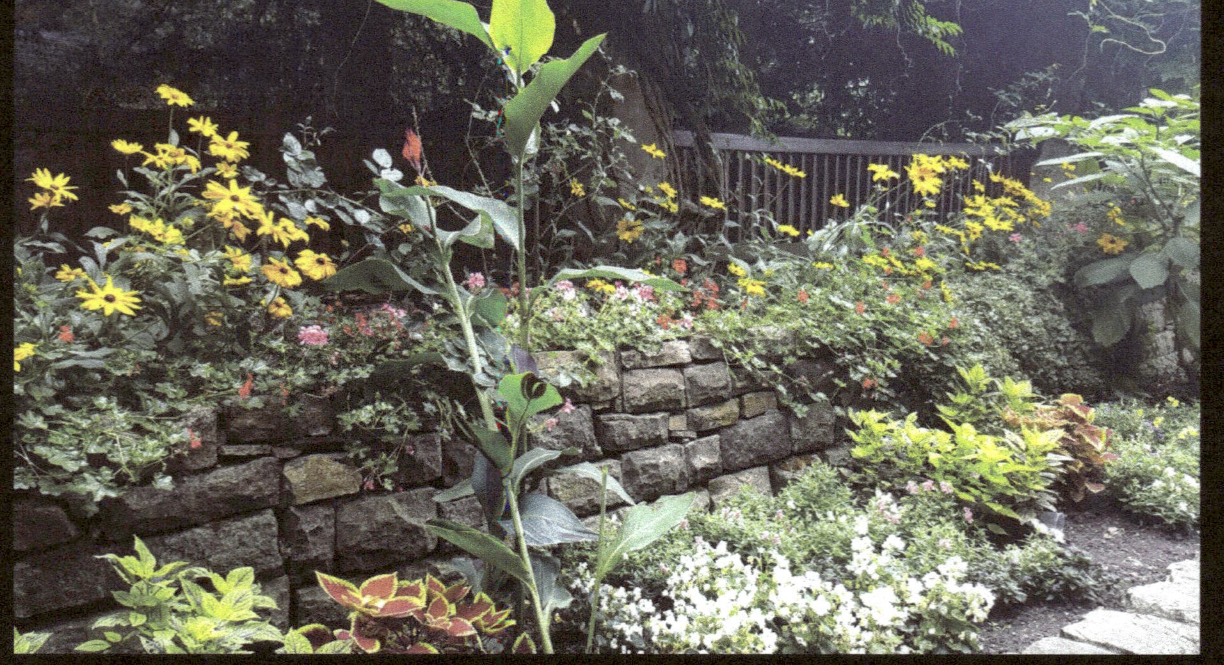

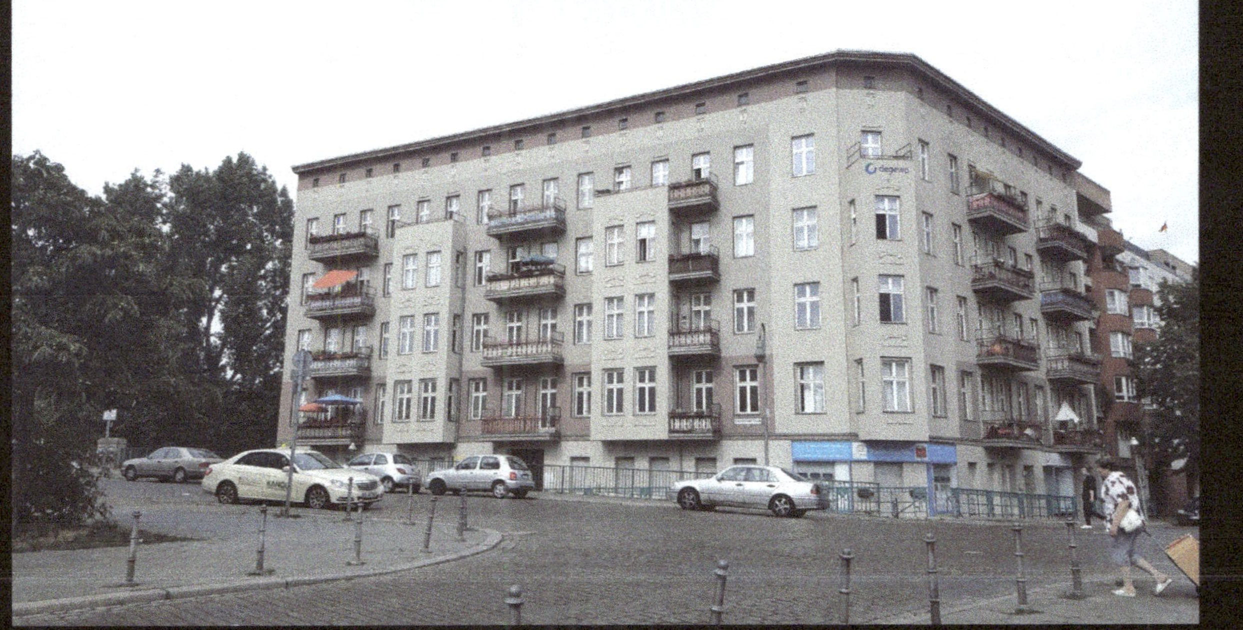

AT THE CORNER

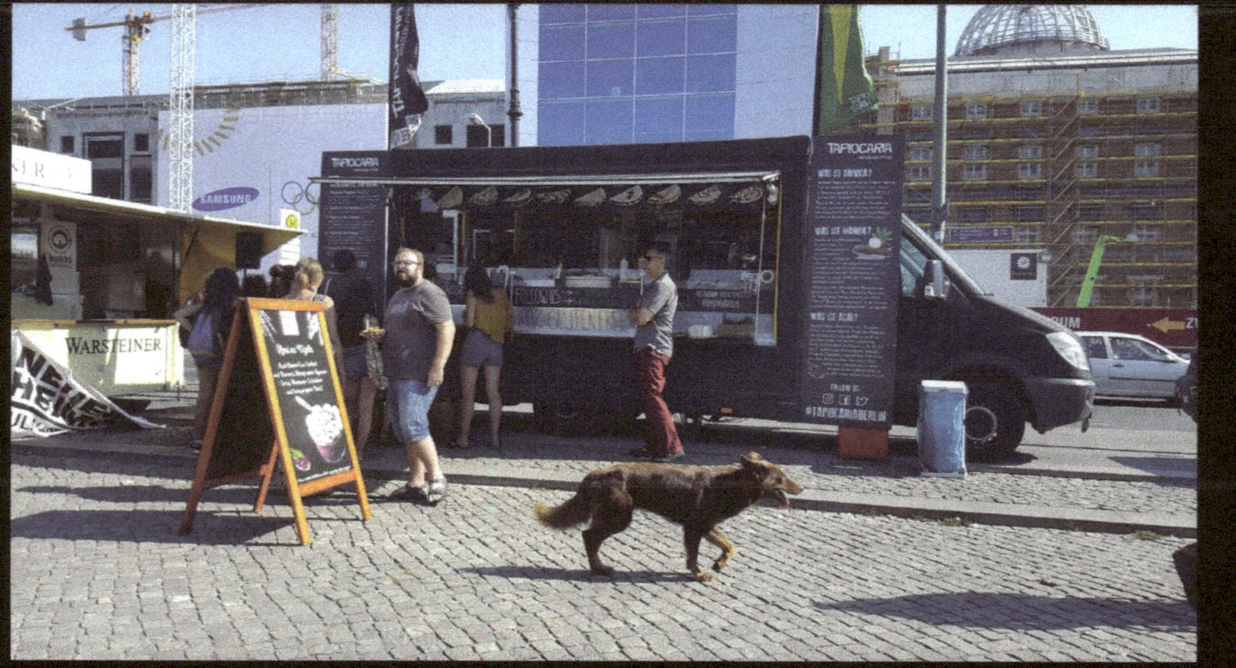

FREEDOM

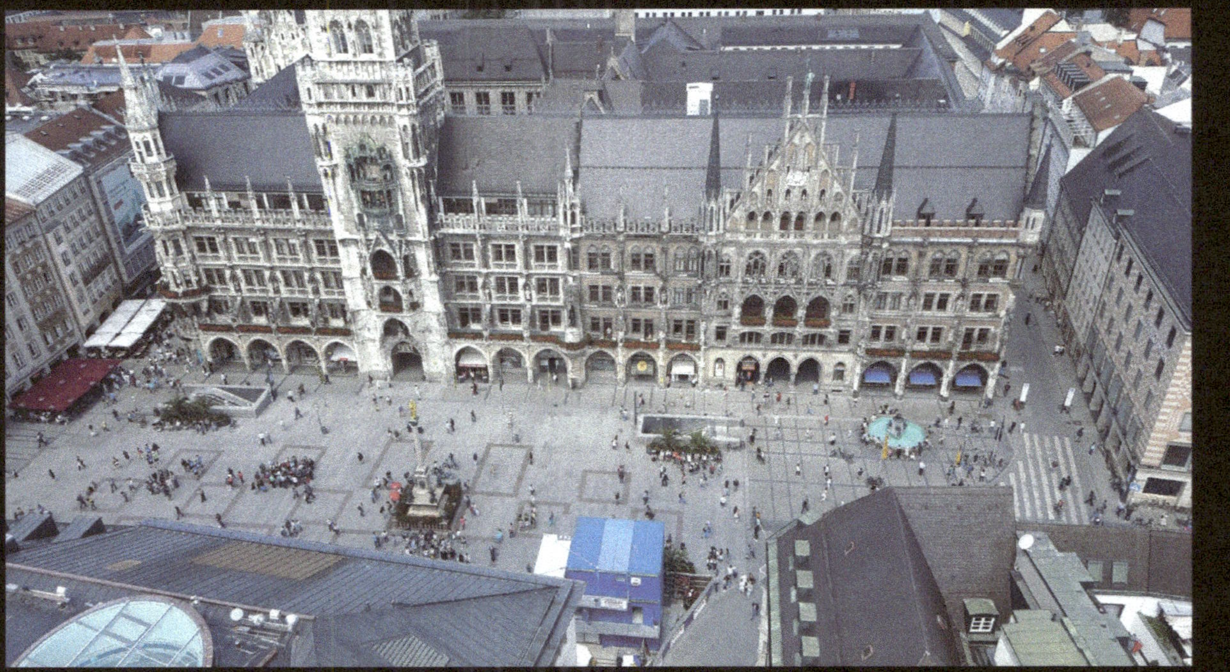

FROM THE BELL TOWER

GRAVE

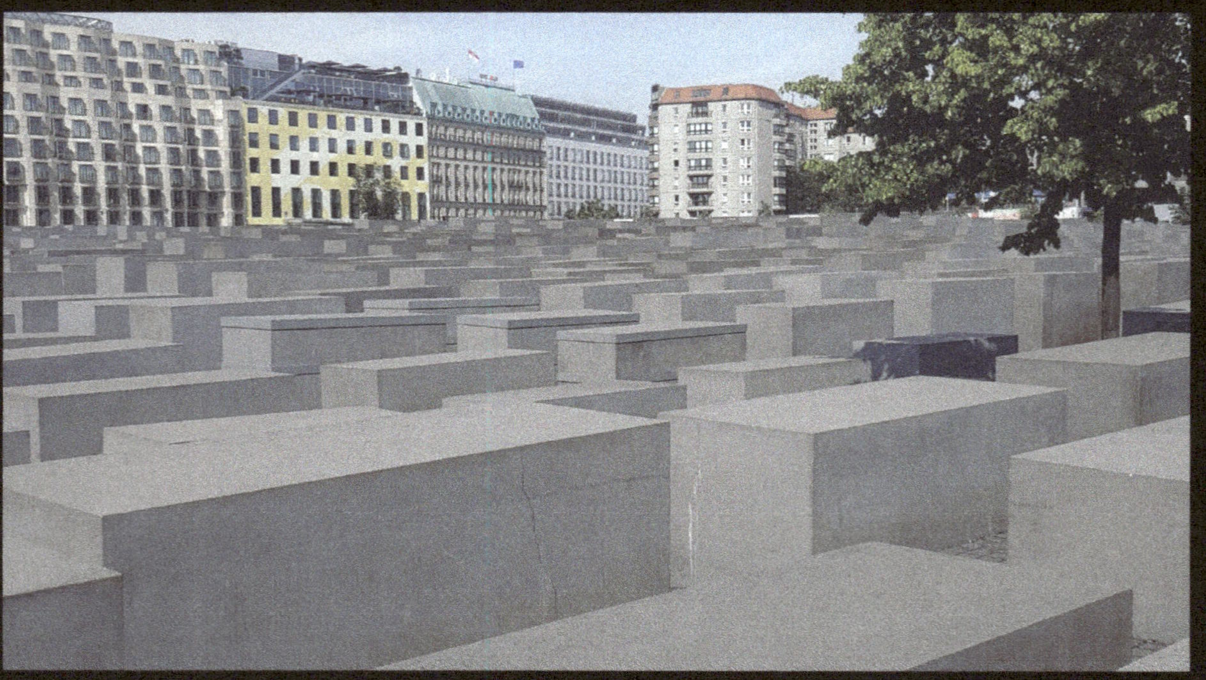

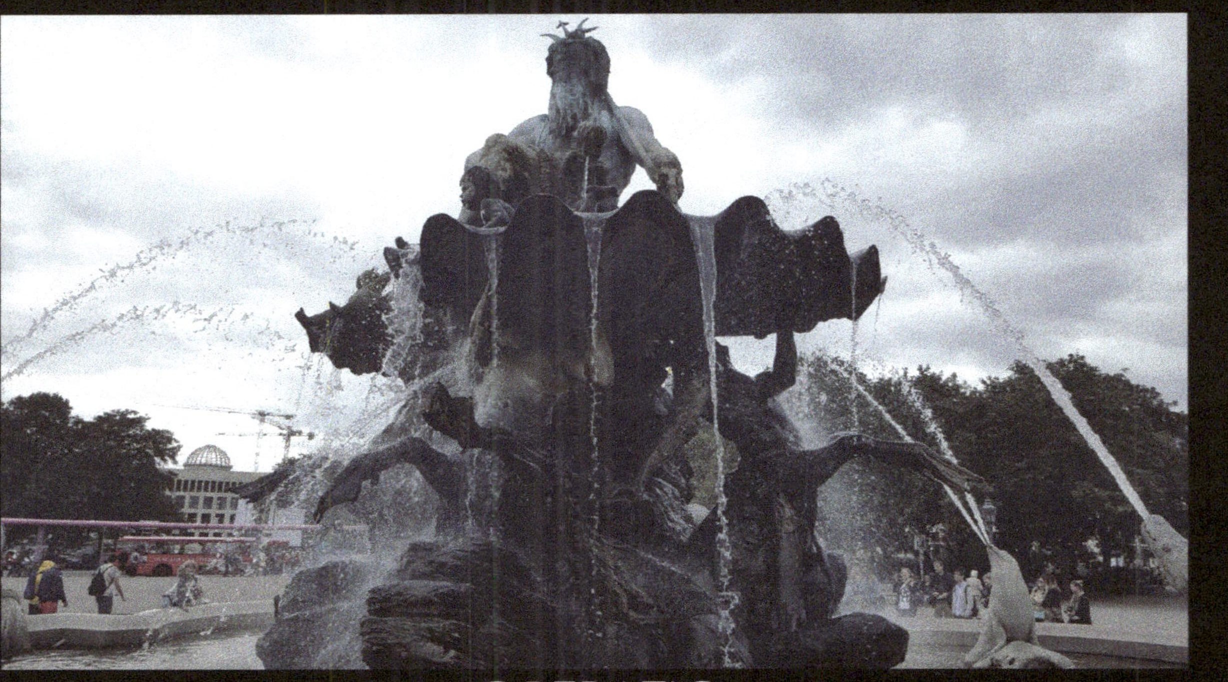

OPERATIC

ON THE HILL

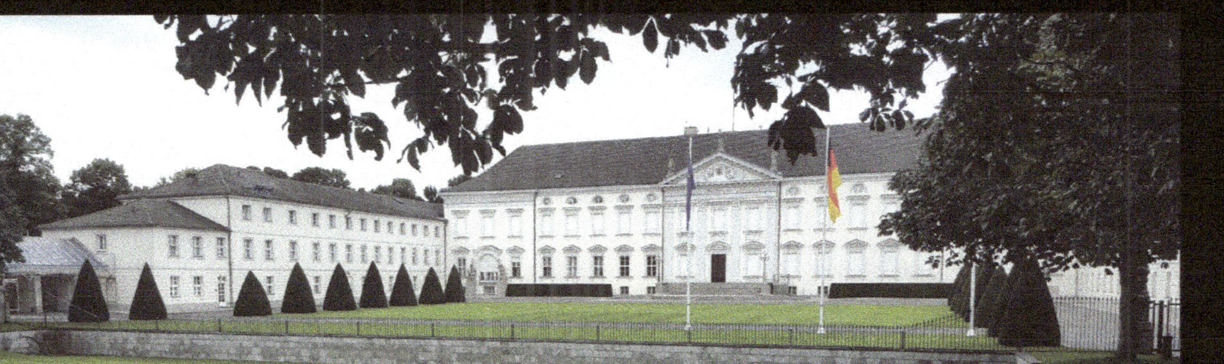
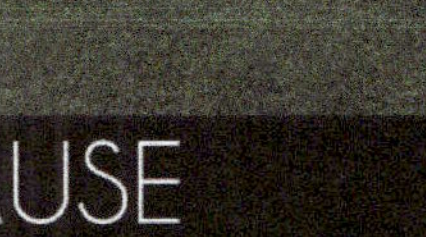

PAUSE

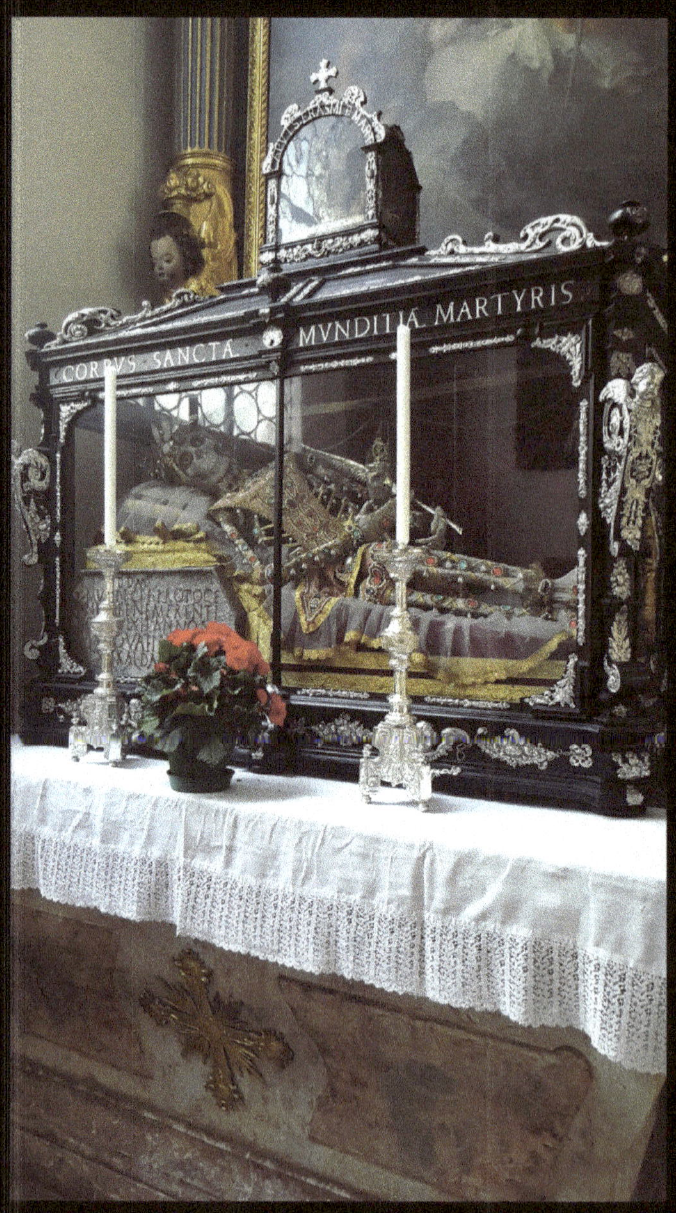

SLEEPING BEAUTY

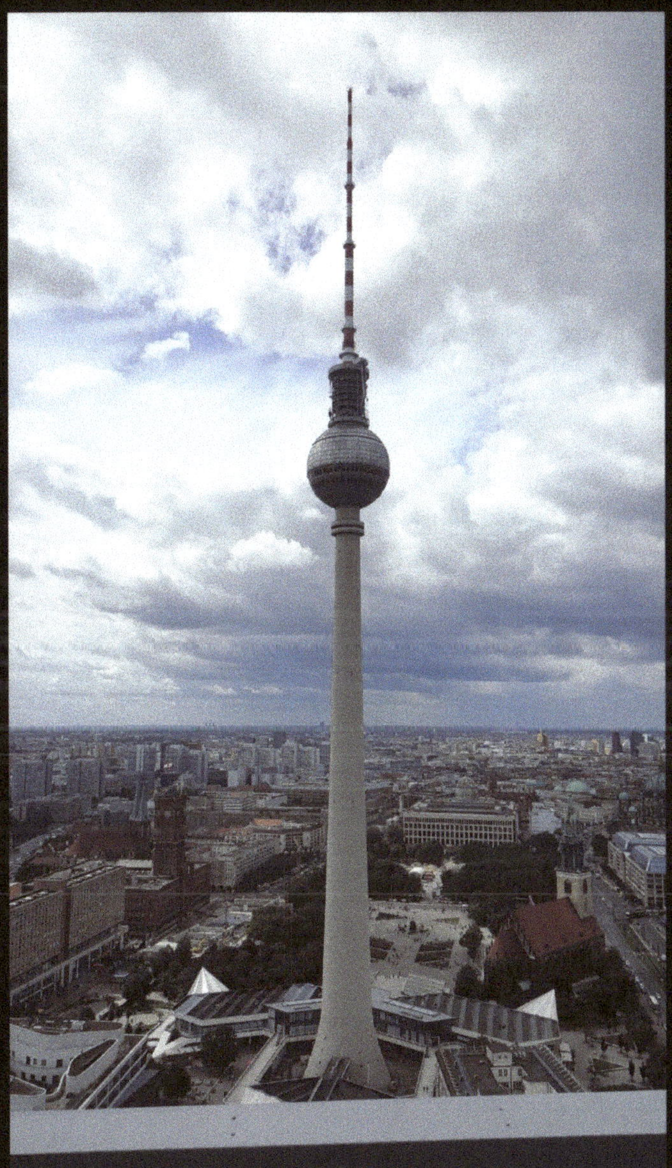

SPIKED CROWN

SPROUTING LIKE WEEDS

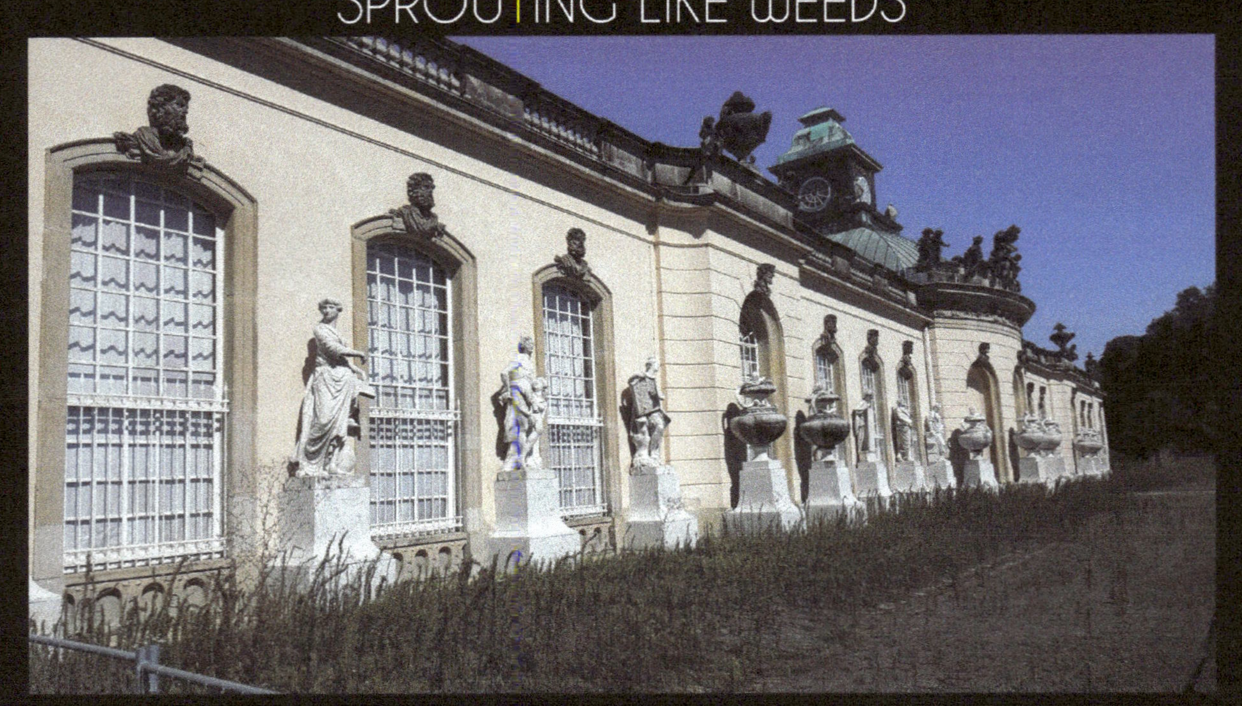

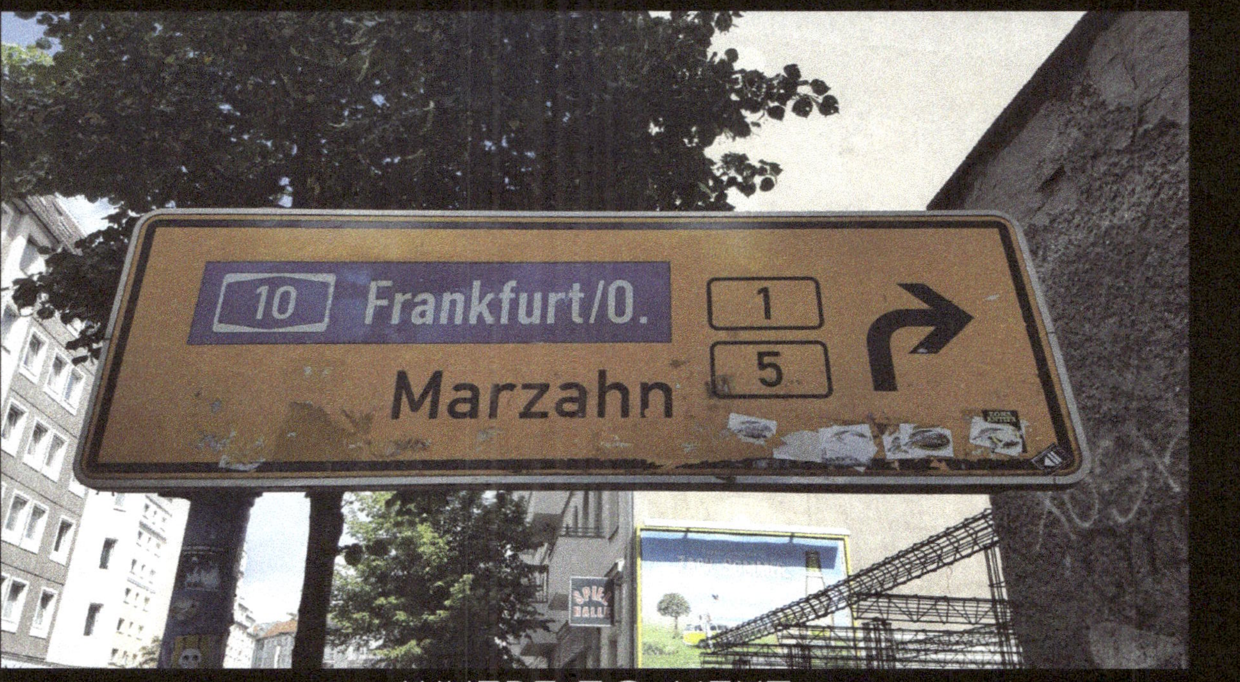
10 Frankfurt/O.
Marzahn
1
5

WHERE TO NEXT

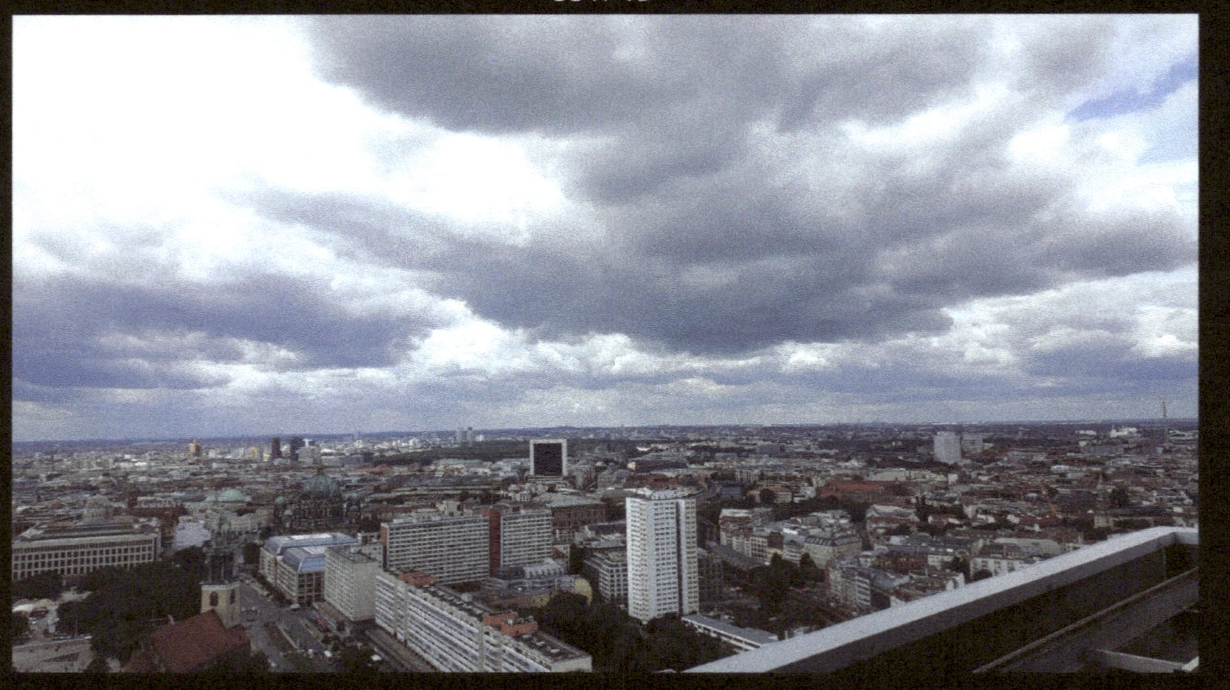
WIND

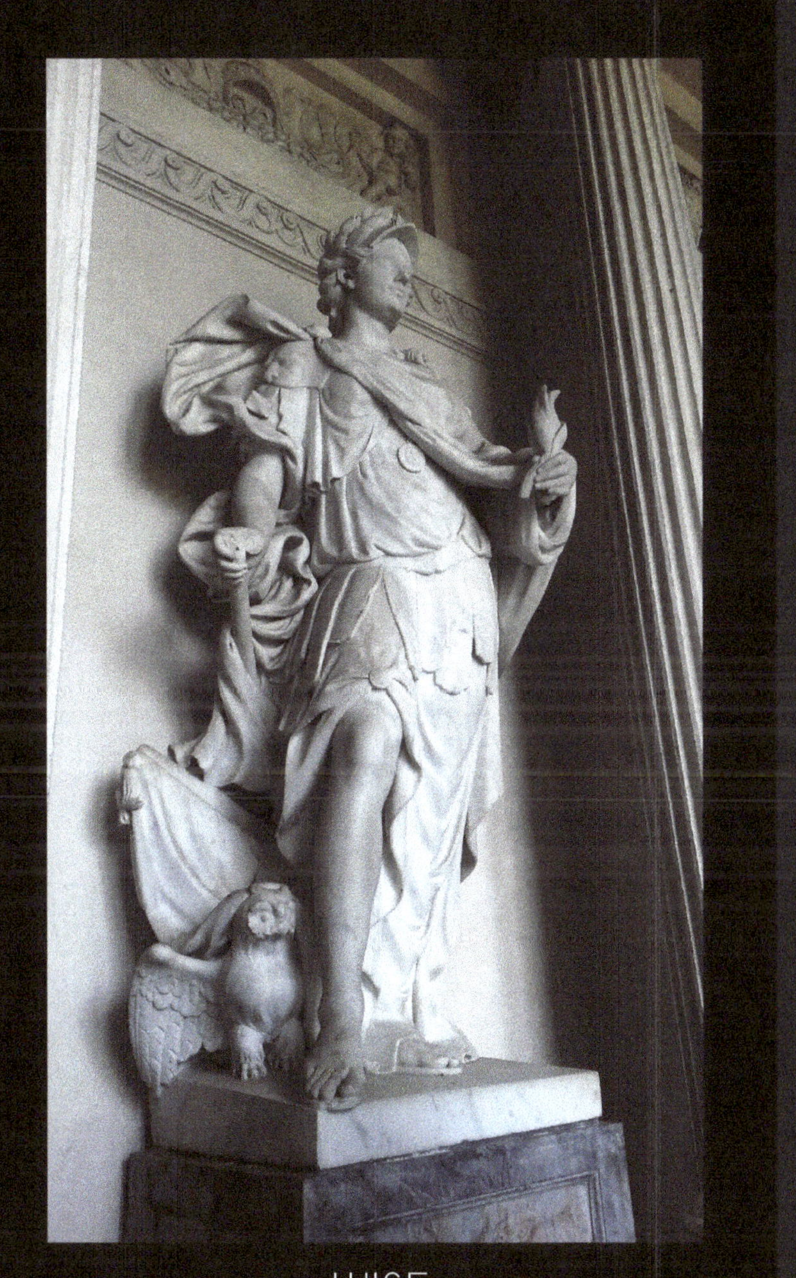

WISE

SIDEWAYS

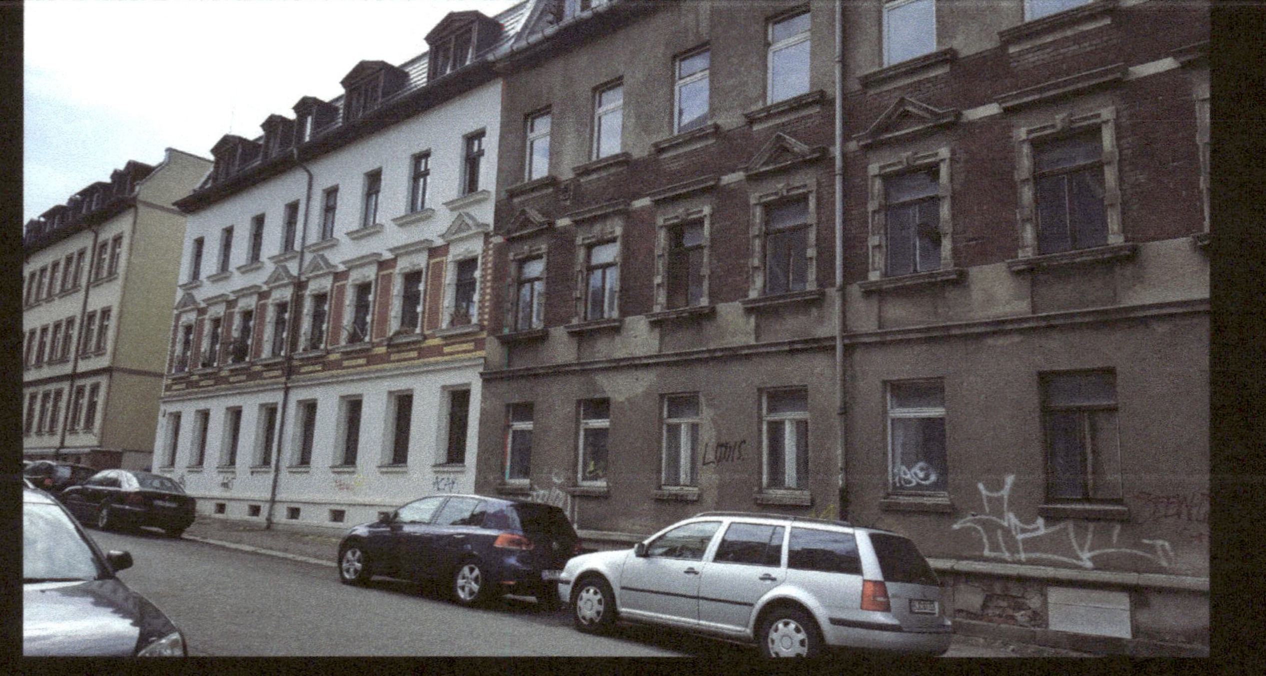

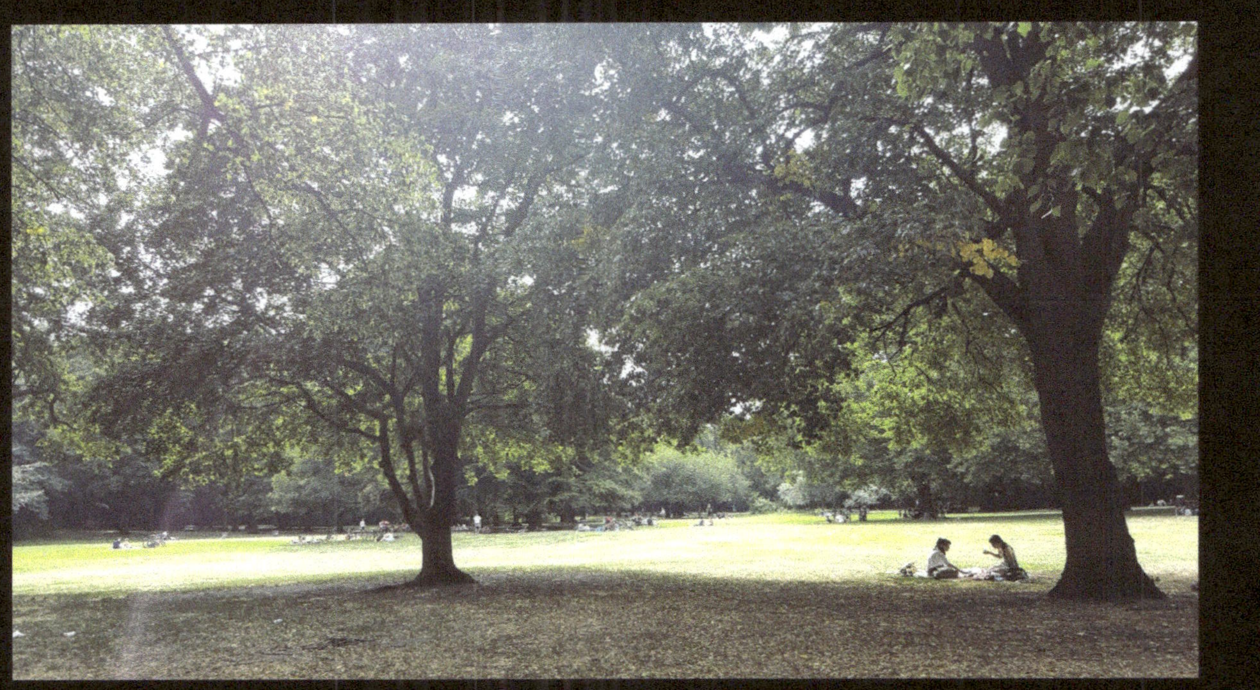
SPARK PARK

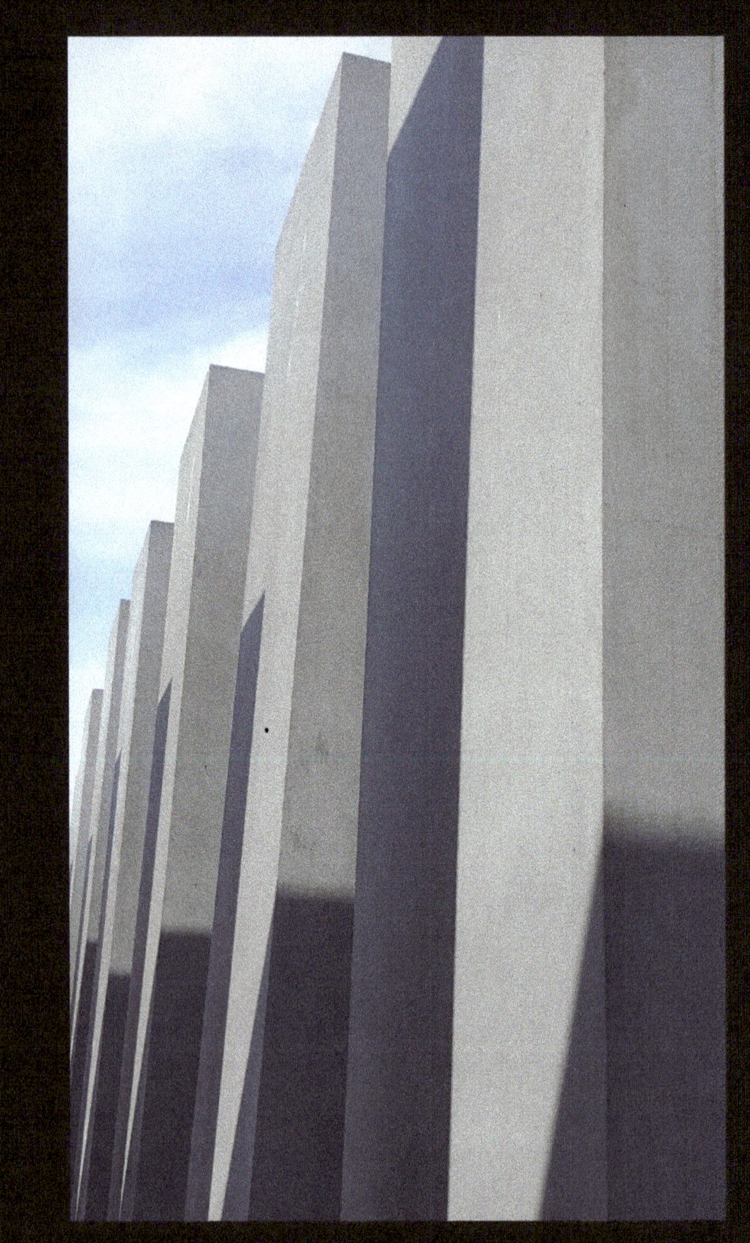

MENHIR

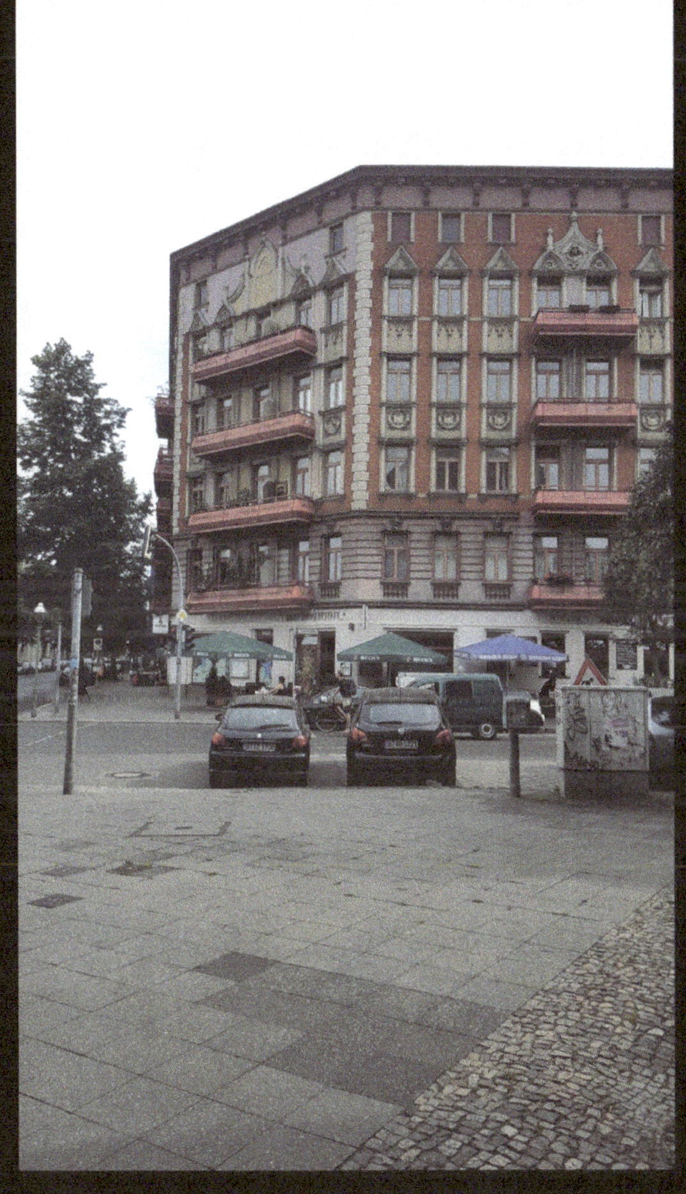

MEET YOU SOON

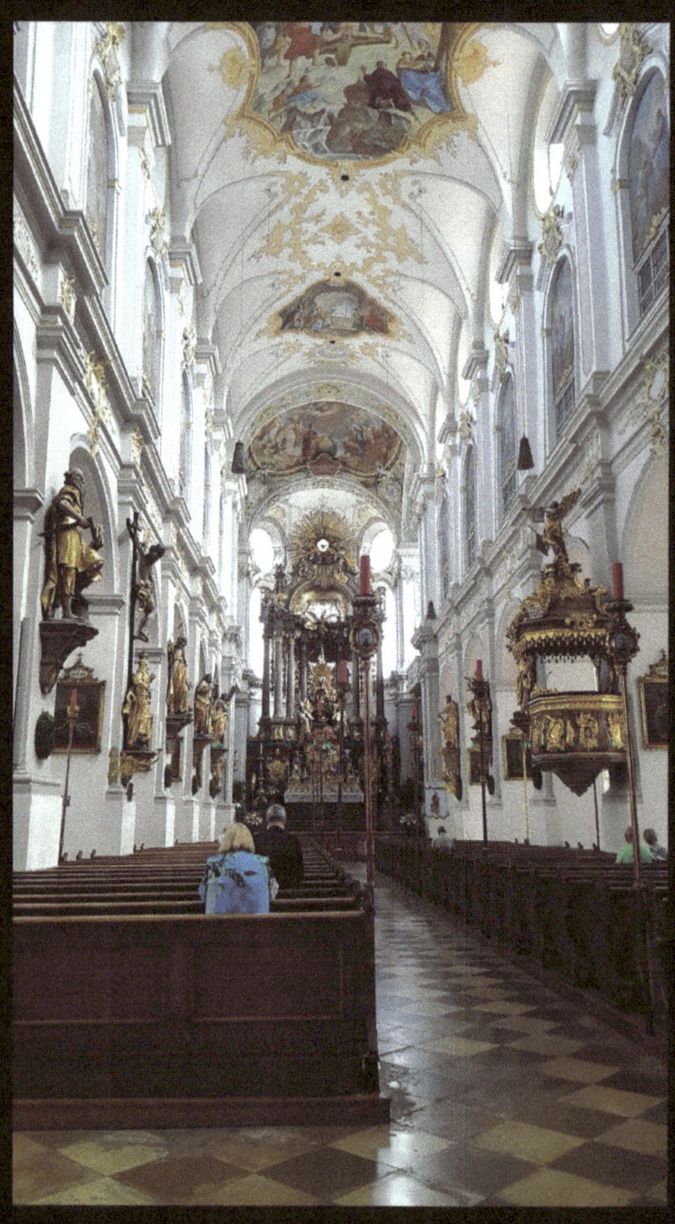

INTIMATE

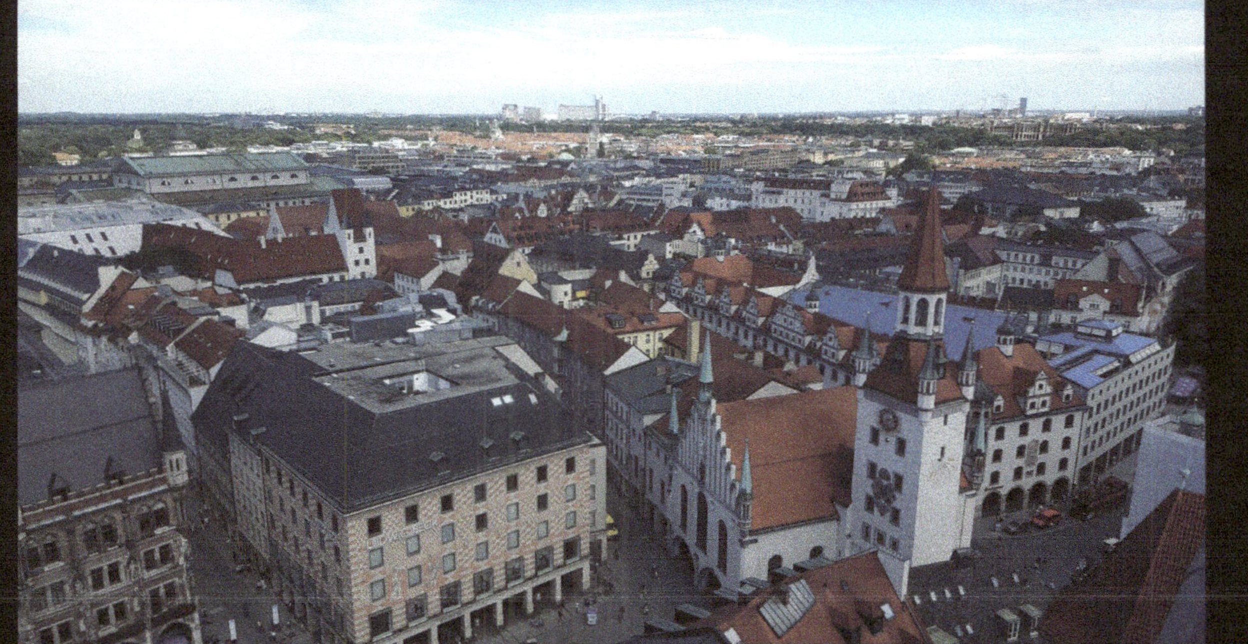
MEDIEVAL

NYMPHEAS

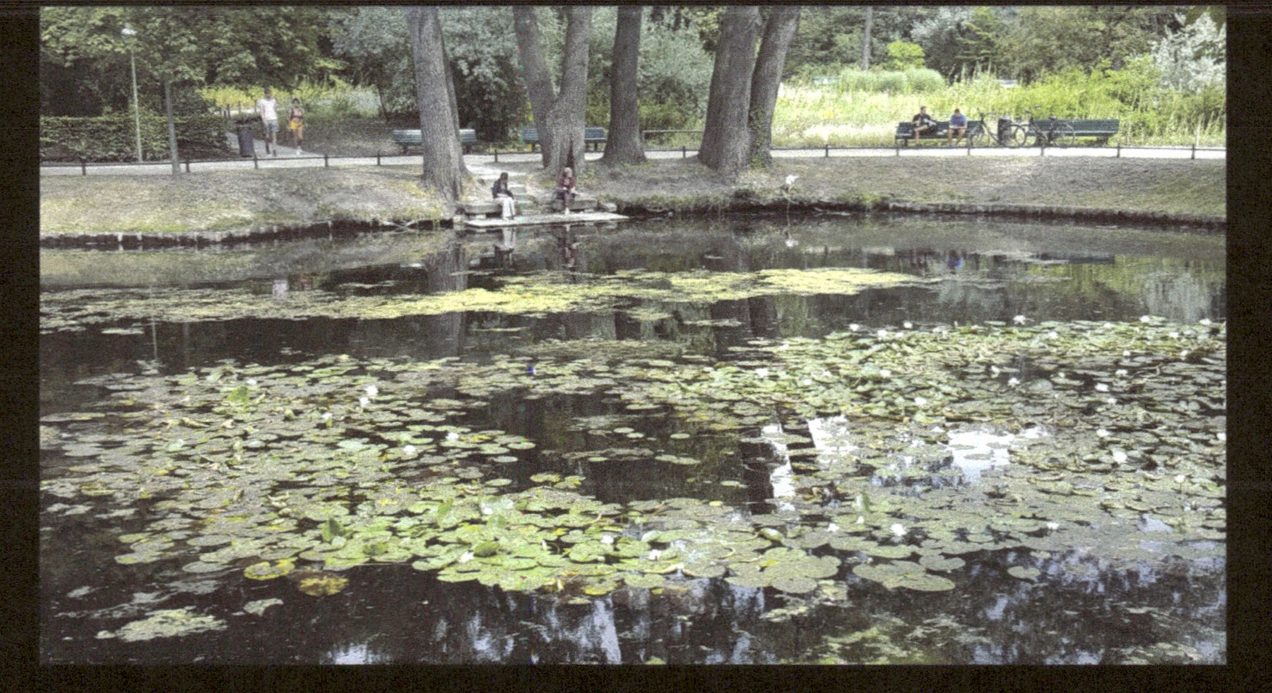

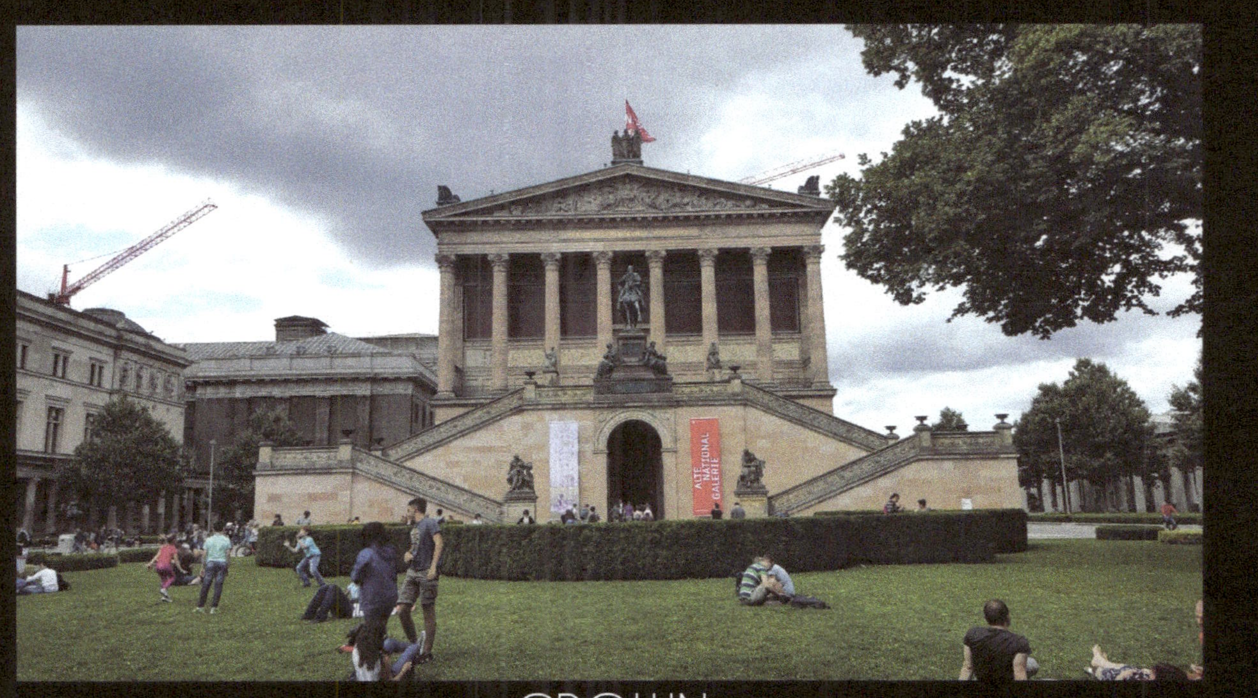

CROWN

RESIST

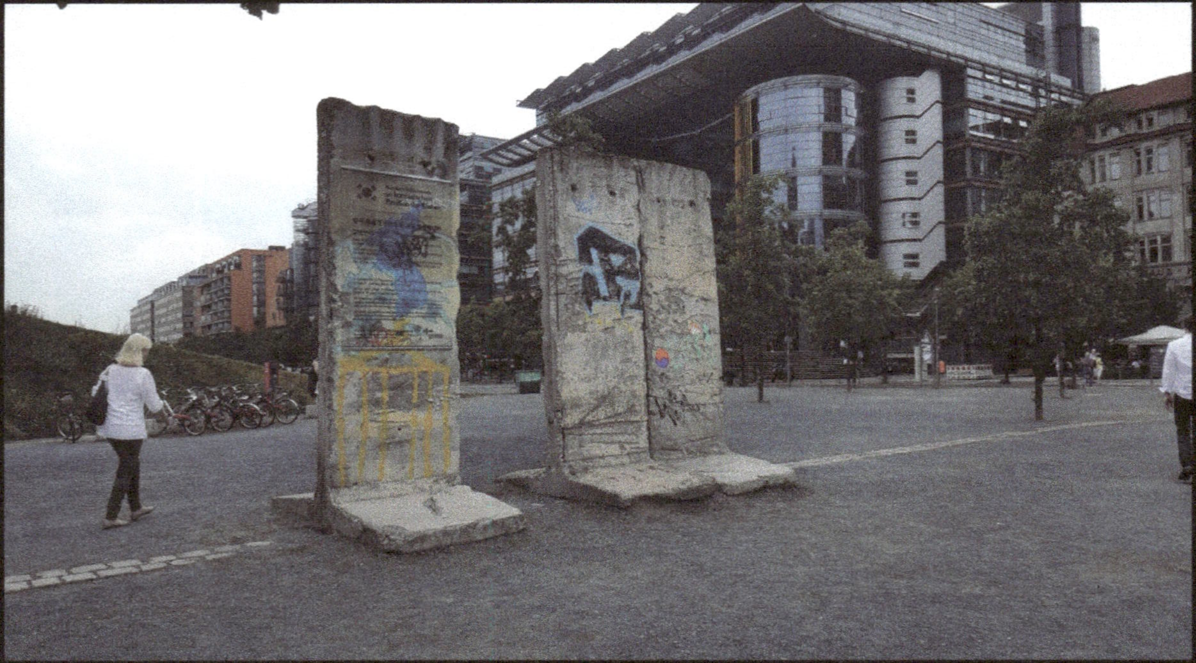

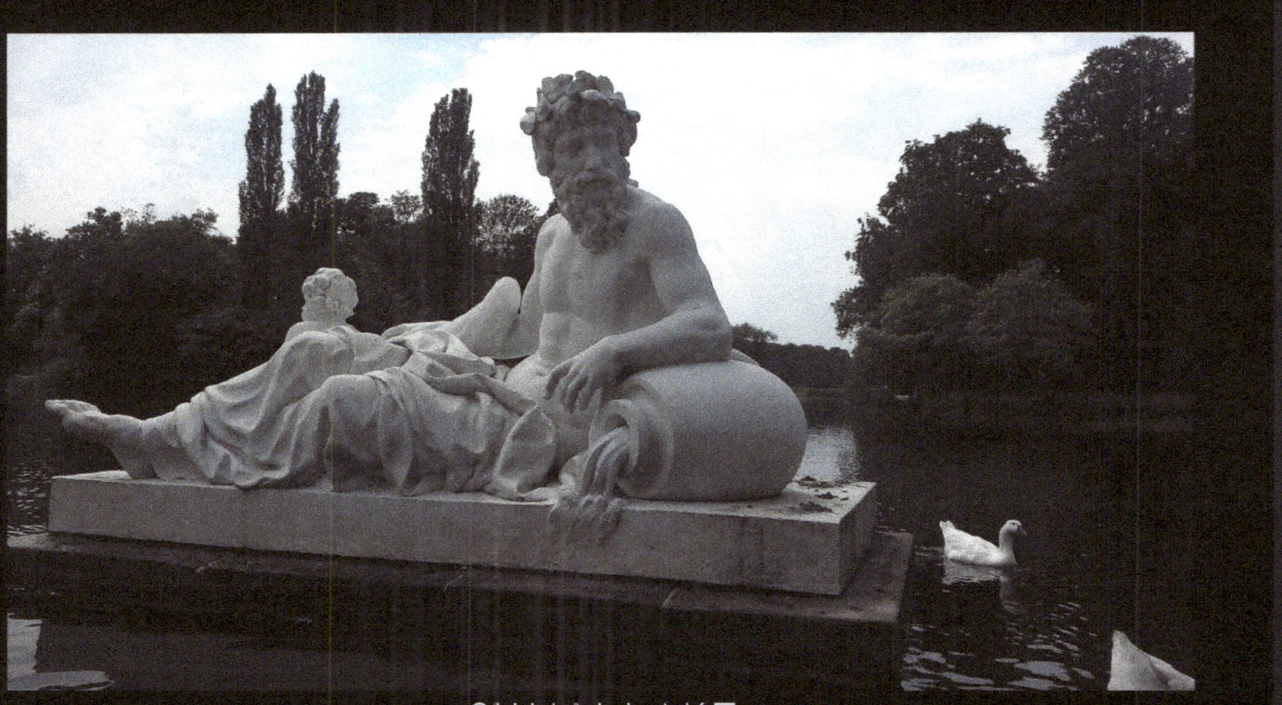
SWAN LAKE

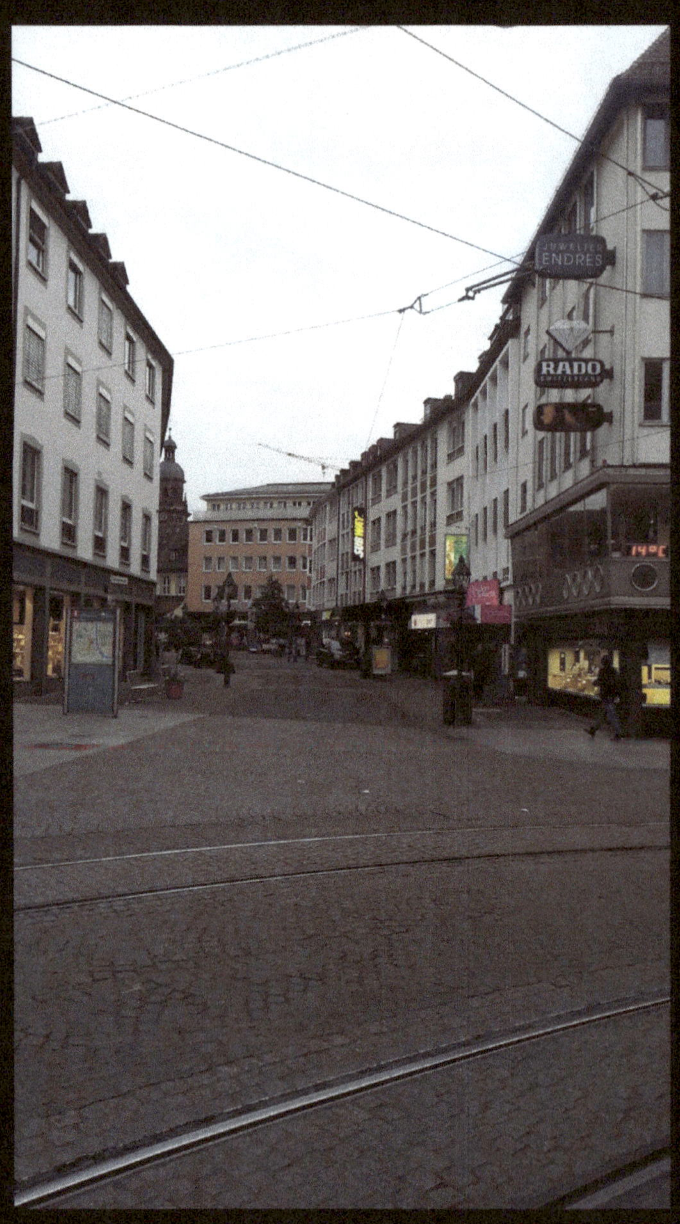

INTERSECTION

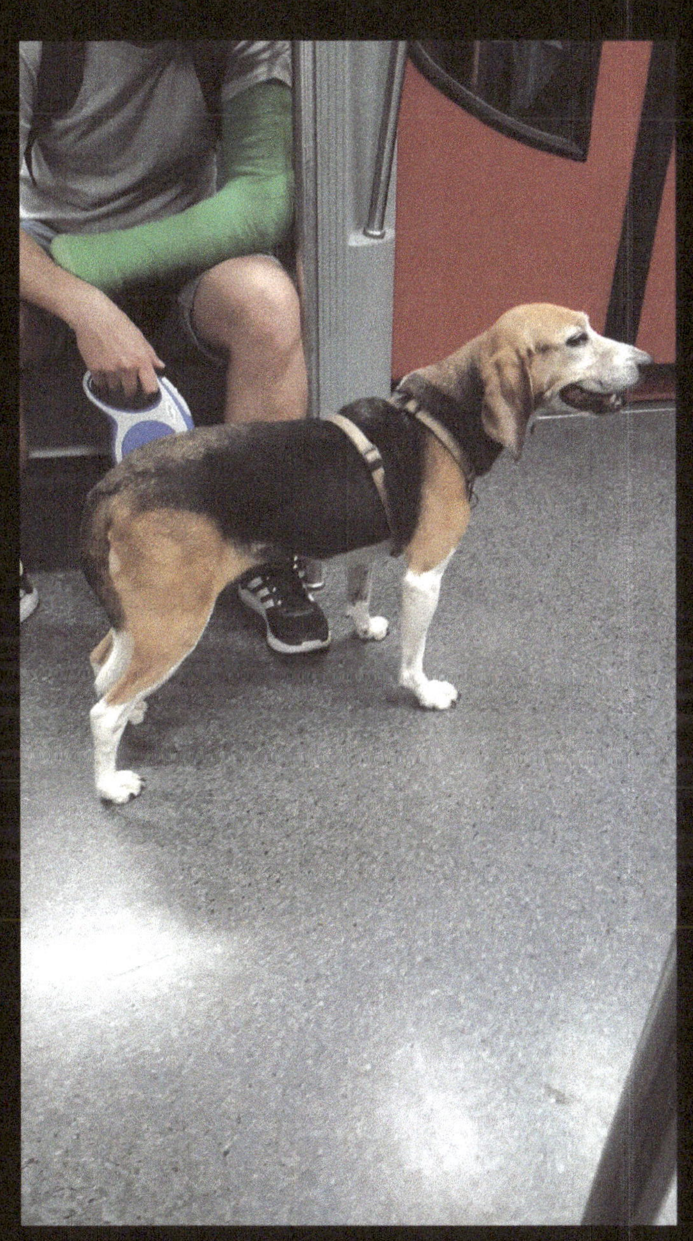

COMMUTER

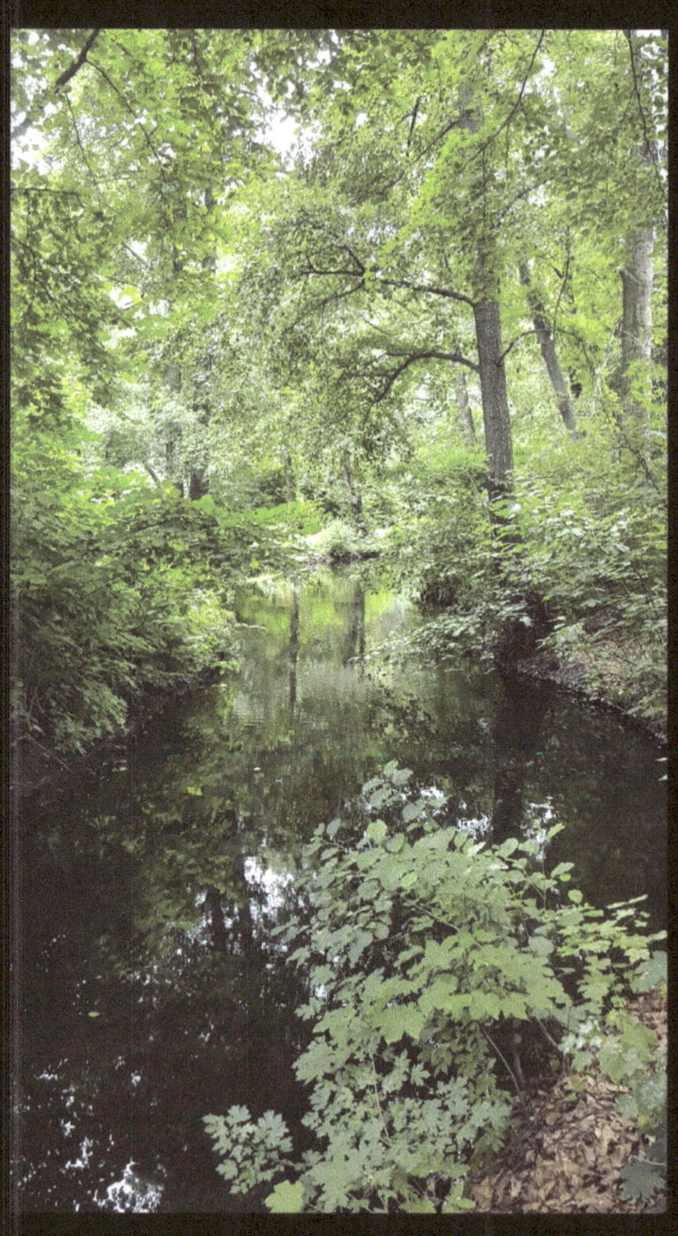

EMERALD BEND

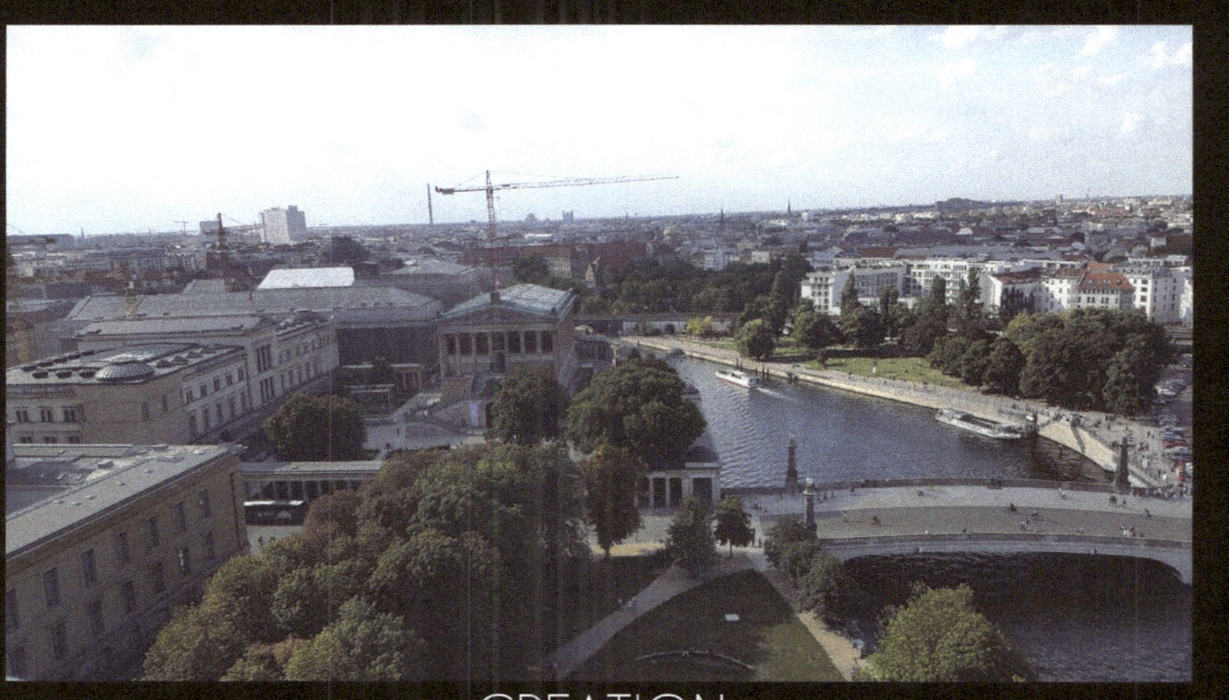
CREATION

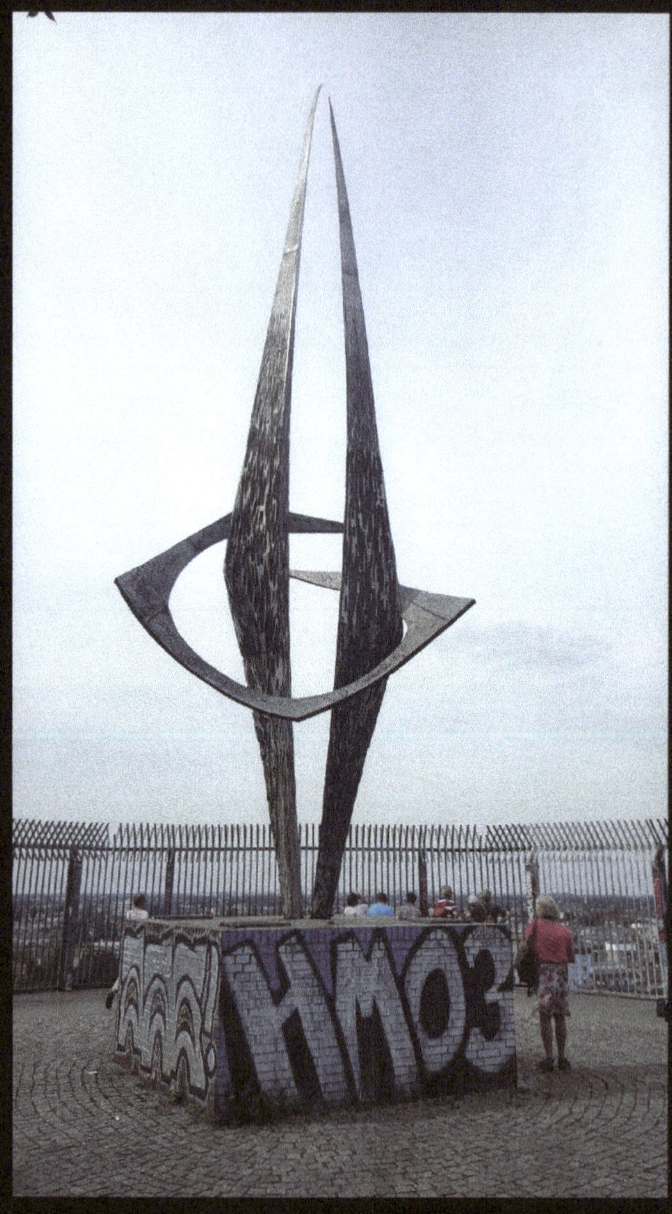

BREACHING

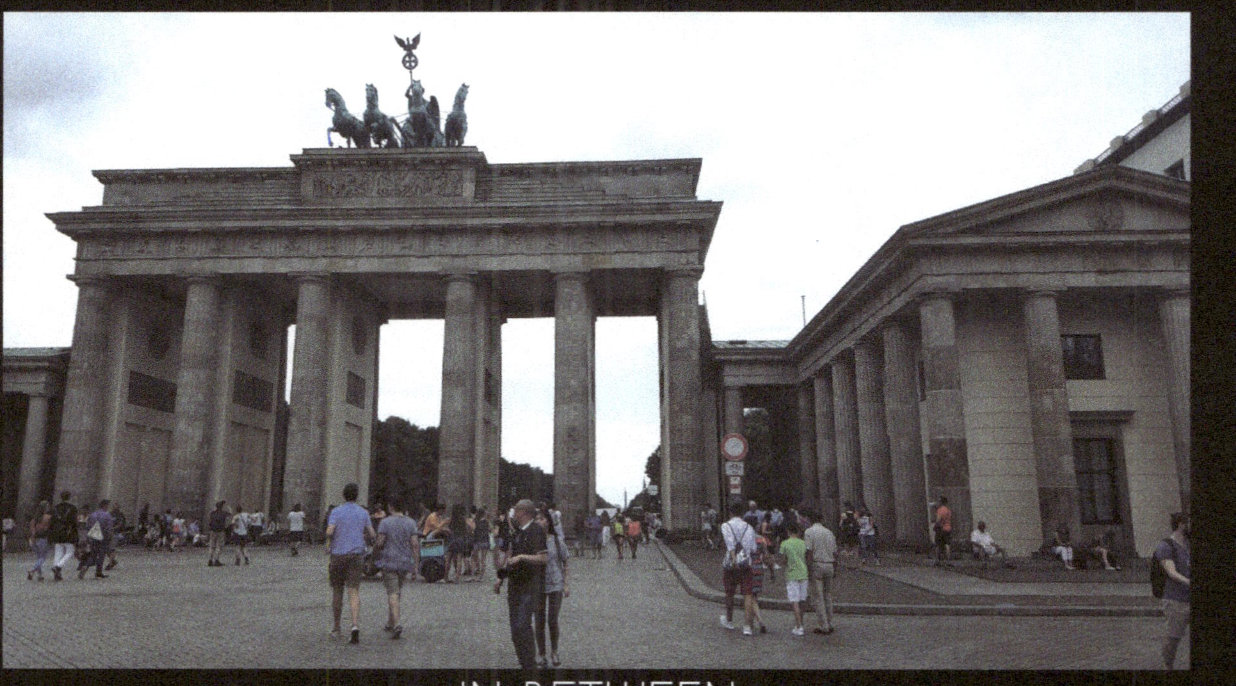
IN BETWEEN

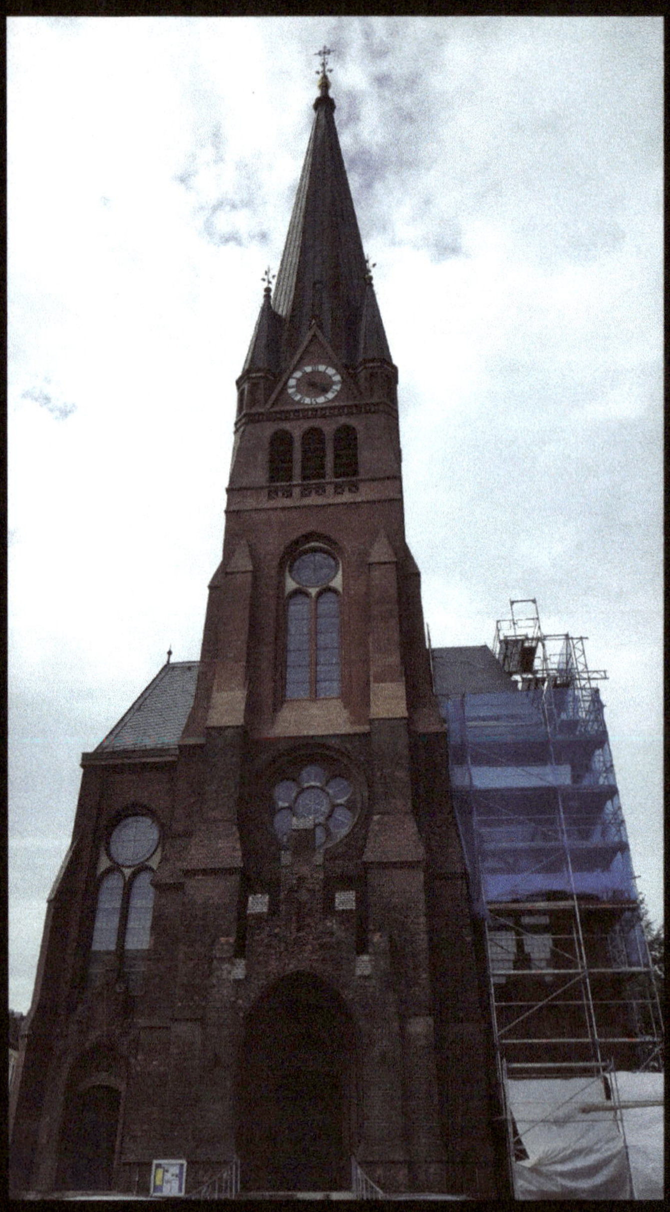

GLOAMING

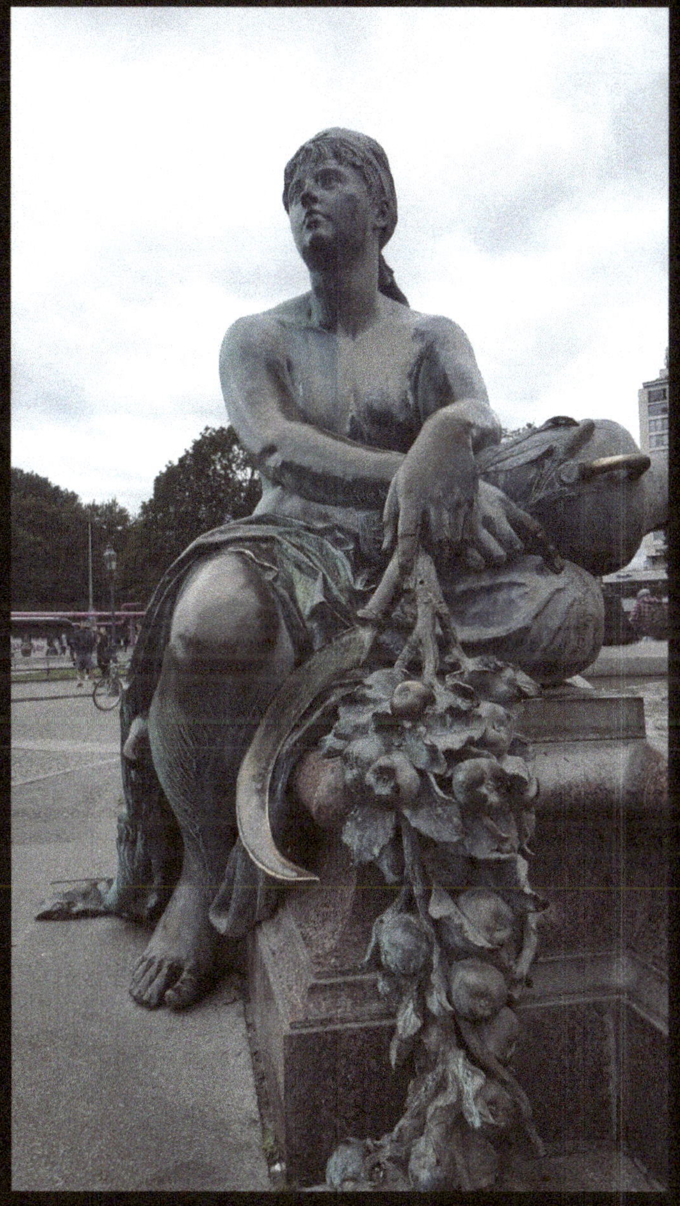

CONTEMPLATE

PINK PICNIC

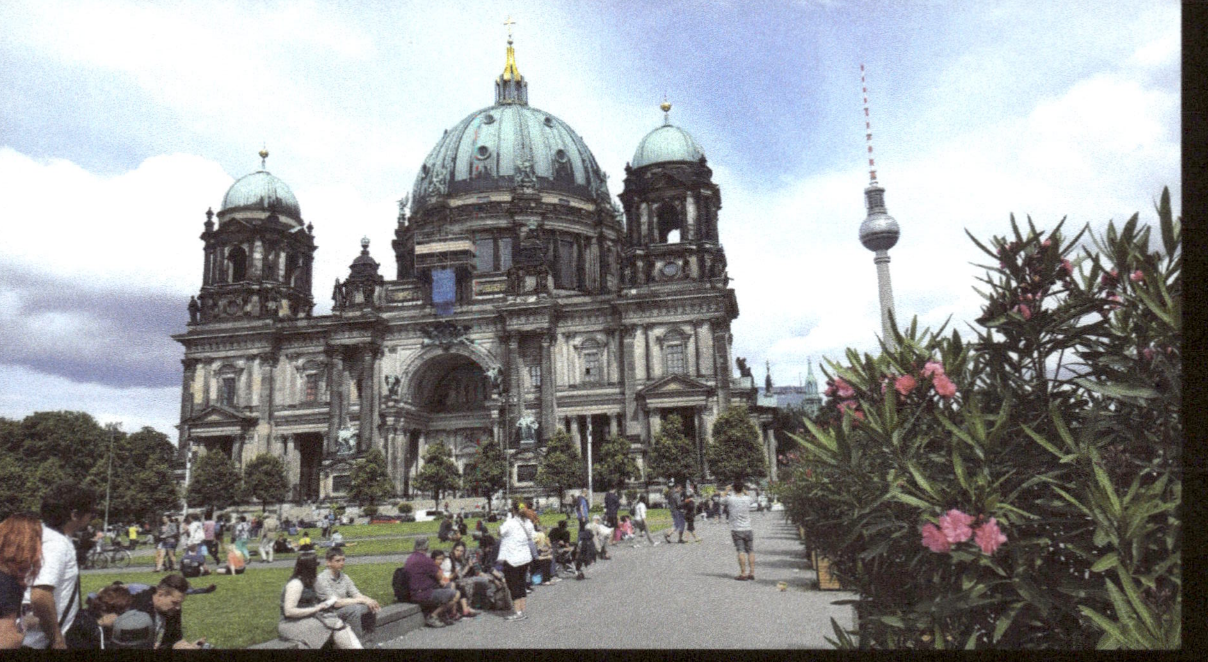

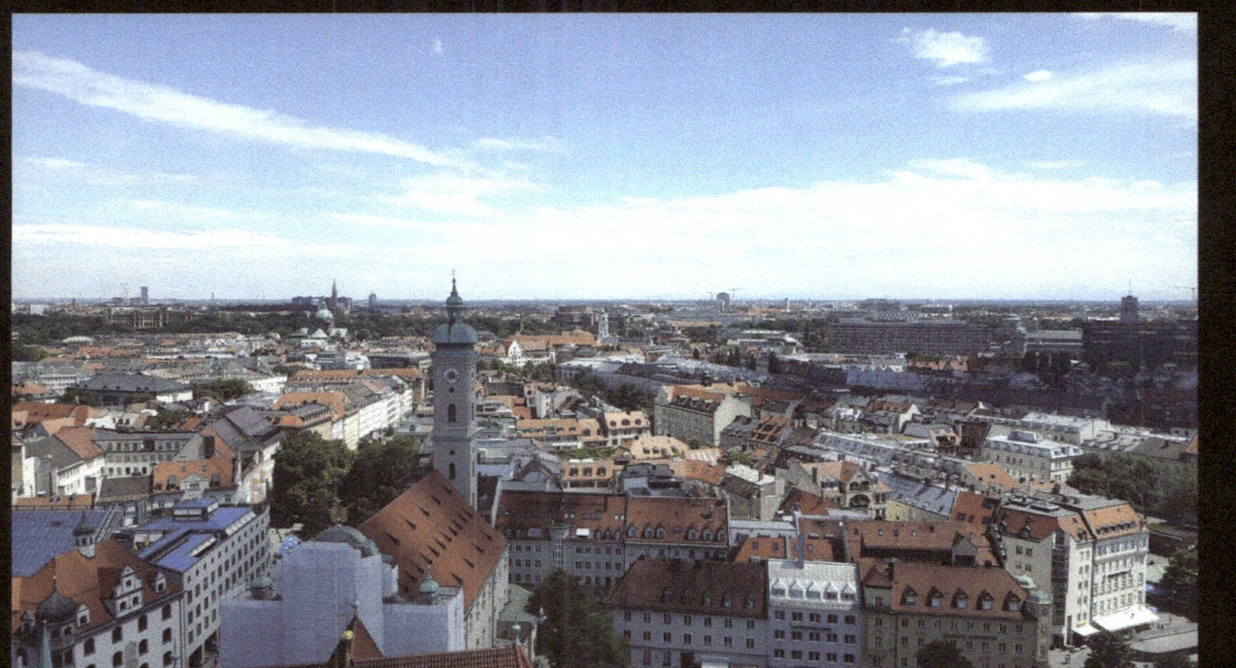

TOWNSCAPE

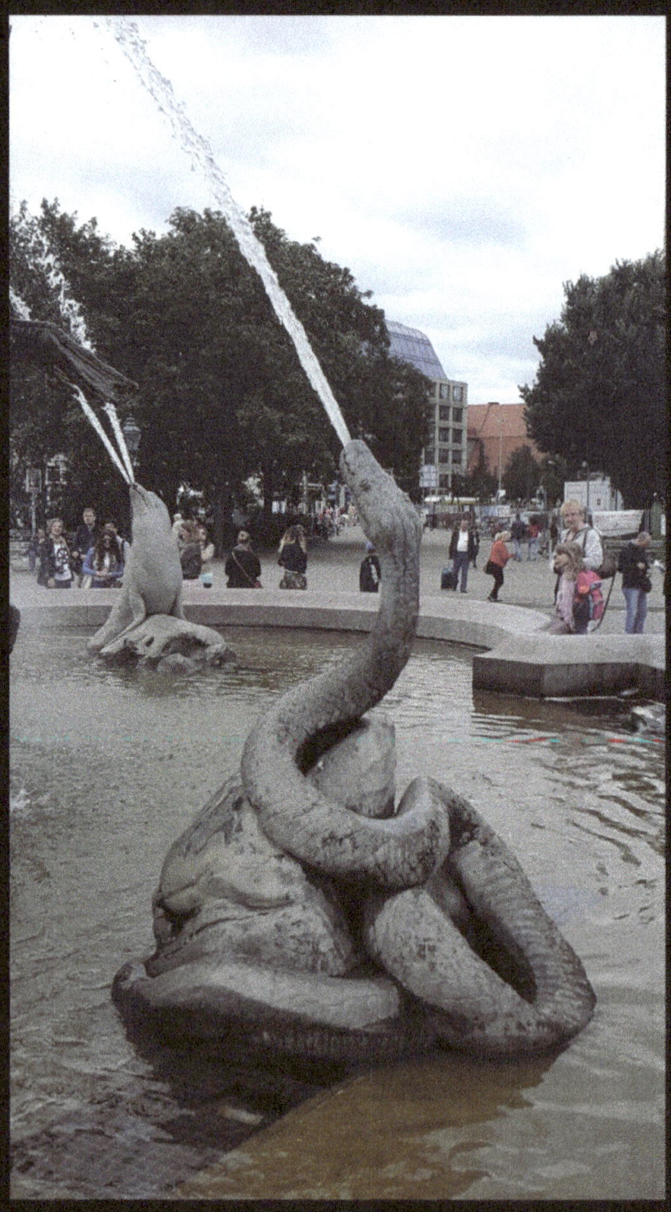

HISS

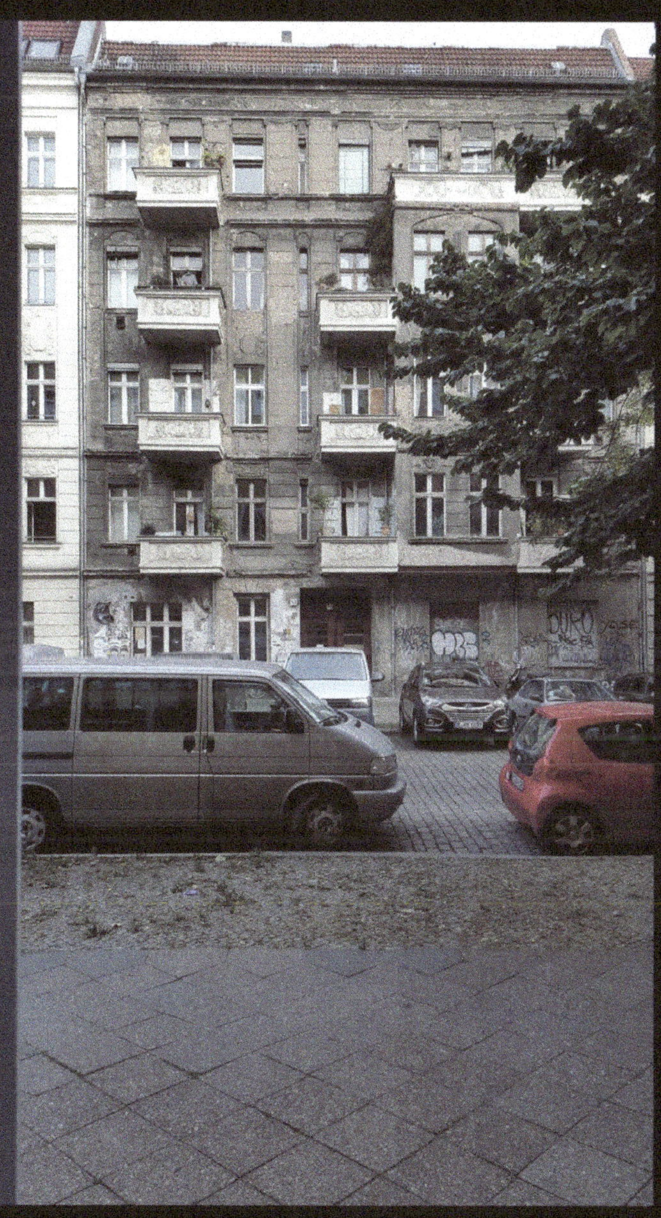

EVERYDAY

AMBLE

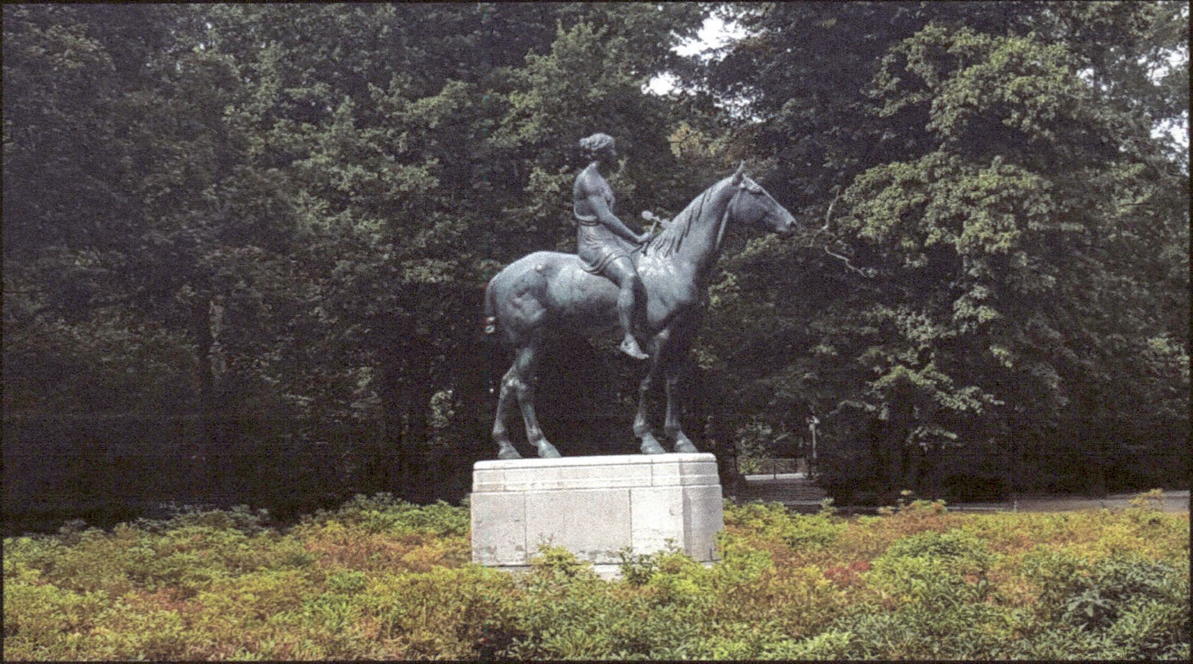

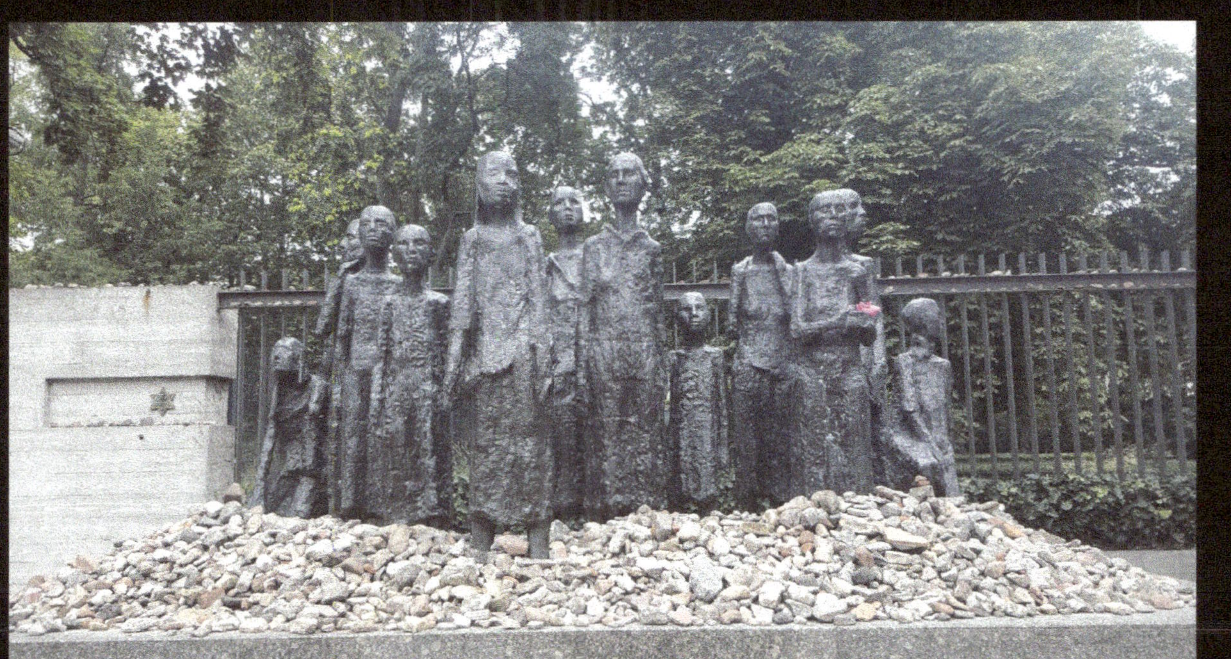
MEMORY NEVER FADES

About the Author

Laine Cunningham is an award-winning novelist. Her women's travel adventure memoir *Woman Alone: A Six-Month Journey Through the Australian Outback* appeals to fans of *Wild* and *Eat Pray Love*.

Fiction

The Family Made of Dust

Beloved

Reparation

Nonfiction

Woman Alone

On the Wallaby Track: Australian Words and Phrases

Seven Sisters: Messages from Aboriginal Australia

Writing While Female or Black or Gay

The Zen of Travel
The Zen of Gardening
Zen in the Stable
The Zen of Chocolate
The Zen of Dogs

The Wisdom of Puppies
The Wisdom of Babies
The Wisdom of Weddings

Bikes of Berlin
Necropolises of New Orleans I & II
Ruins of Rome I & II
Ancients of Assisi I & II
Panoramas of Portugal
Nuances of New York
Glimpses of Germany
Impressions of Italy
Utopia of the Unicorn